# Enrolled Agent University

## Representation Tax Law

## Certifyible.com

# GRAB THE ONLINE COURSE

Go to **www.certifyible.com** to grab the online course that has training videos, additional pop quizzes, and a final exam test bank to test your knowledge.

# CONTENTS

# Practice Before The IRS

## Overview

The Office of Professional Responsibility generally has responsibility for matters related to practitioner conduct, and exclusive responsibility for discipline, including disciplinary proceedings and sanctions. The Return Preparer Office is responsible for matters related to the issuance of PTINs, acting on applications for enrollment and administering competency testing and continuing education for designated groups.

## What Is Practice Before the IRS?

Circular 230 covers all matters relating to any of the following:

• Communicating with the IRS on behalf of a taxpayer regarding the taxpayer's rights, privileges, or liabilities under laws and regulations administered by the IRS.

• Representing a taxpayer at conferences, hearings, or meetings with the IRS.

• Preparing, filing or submitting documents, or advising on the preparation, filing or submission of documents, including tax returns, with the IRS on behalf of a taxpayer.

• Providing a client with written tax advice on one or more Federal tax matters.

Any individual may for compensation prepare or assist with the preparation of a tax return or claim for refund, appear as a witness for a taxpayer before the IRS, or furnish information at the request of the IRS or any of its officers or employees.

An example of practice before the IRS would be a scenario where a tax attorney, John, is representing a client, Sarah, who is being audited by the Internal Revenue Service (IRS). John engages in various activities that fall under the definition of practice before the IRS, as outlined in Circular 230.

First, John communicates with the IRS on behalf of Sarah regarding her rights, privileges, and liabilities under the relevant tax laws and regulations. He discusses Sarah's tax situation, presents supporting documents, and provides explanations to address any concerns raised by the IRS during the audit process.

Next, John represents Sarah at a conference with the IRS. He attends a meeting with the IRS auditors to discuss the findings of the audit, present additional evidence, and negotiate on Sarah's behalf to reach a favorable resolution.

In addition to representing Sarah, John assists her with the preparation and filing of necessary documents, including her tax returns. He reviews Sarah's financial records, identifies eligible deductions and credits, and advises her on proper compliance with tax laws to ensure accurate reporting.

Furthermore, John provides written tax advice to Sarah on specific federal tax matters. He prepares a detailed memorandum outlining the potential tax consequences of certain financial decisions, such as the tax implications of selling an investment property or starting a new business.
This advice helps Sarah make informed decisions and minimizes the risk of non-compliance.

In this example, John's activities, which involve communicating with the IRS, representing Sarah at meetings, preparing and filing documents, and providing written tax advice, all fall within the scope of practice before the IRS as defined by Circular 230.

**Who Can Practice Before the IRS?**

The following individuals are subject to the Regulations contained in Circular 230:

- Appraisers
- Attorneys
- Certified Public Accountants (CPAs)
- Enrolled Agents
- Enrolled Retirement Plan Agents
- Enrolled Actuaries Low Income Taxpayer Clinic Student Interns
- Unenrolled Return Preparers

However, any individual who is authorized generally to practice (a recognized representative) must be designated as the taxpayer's representative and file a written declaration with the IRS stating that he or she is authorized and qualified to represent a particular taxpayer. Form 2848 can be used for this purpose.

## Enrolled Practitioners

### Appraisers

Any individual who prepares appraisals supporting the valuation of assets in connection with one or more federal tax matters is subject to the regulations contained in Circular 230. Appraisers have no representation rights but may appear as witnesses on behalf of taxpayers.

### Attorneys

Any attorney who is not currently under suspension or debarment from practice before the IRS and who is a member in good standing of the bar of the highest court of any U.S. state, possession, territory, commonwealth, or the District of Columbia may practice before the IRS.

### Certified public accountants (CPAs)

Any CPA who is not currently under suspension or debarment from practice before the IRS and who is duly qualified to practice as a CPA in any U.S. state, possession, territory, commonwealth, or the District of Columbia may practice before the IRS.

### Enrolled agents

Any enrolled agent with active status who is not currently under suspension or debarment from practice before the IRS may practice before the IRS.

### Enrolled retirement plan agents

Any enrolled retirement plan agent in active status who is not currently under suspension or debarment from practice before the IRS may practice before the IRS. The practice of enrolled retirement plan agents is limited to certain Internal Revenue Code sections that relate to their area of expertise, principally those sections governing employee retirement plans.

## Enrolled actuaries

Any individual who is enrolled as an actuary by the Joint Board for the Enrollment of Actuaries who is not currently under suspension or debarment from practice before the IRS may practice before the IRS. The practice of enrolled actuaries is limited to certain Internal Revenue Code sections that relate to their area of expertise, principally those sections governing employee retirement plans.

## Annual Filing Season Program

The Annual Filing Season Program is a voluntary program designed to encourage non-credentialed tax return preparers to participate in continuing education (CE) courses.

Non-credentialed return preparers can elect to voluntarily demonstrate completion of basic 1040 filing season tax preparation and other tax law training through continuing education.

Return preparers who complete the requirements for the Annual Filing Season Program will be issued a Record of Completion that they can display and use to differentiate themselves in the marketplace if desired.

Preparers who participate are also included in a public database on IRS.gov that taxpayers use when searching for qualified tax return preparers. The Directory of Federal Tax Return Preparers with Credentials and Select Qualifications only includes attorneys, certified public accountants (CPAs), enrolled agents, enrolled retirement plan agents (ERPAs), enrolled actuaries, and individuals who have received an Annual Filing Season Program – Record of Completion.

A prospective participant must plan and obtain the necessary continuing education before the beginning of the year they want to participate.

For example, to receive a Record of Completion for filing season 2025, all continuing education must be finished by December 31, 2024. Participants must also have an active Preparer Tax Identification Number (PTIN) for the year of participation. And they are required to consent to the following statement:

*I agree to abide by the duties and restrictions relating to practice before the IRS in subpart B and section 10.51 of Treasury Department Circular No. 230 for the entire period covered by the Record of Completion. I understand that failing to comply with the duties and restrictions relating to practice before the IRS in these sections may result in the revocation of my Annual Filing Season Program – Record of Completion, and I may be prohibited from participating in the Annual Filing Season Program in the future.*

Depending on certain factors, a tax return preparer will need either 15 or 18 hours of continuing education from an IRS approved continuing education provider. The following categories need 15 hours annually:

1. Anyone who passed the Registered Tax Return Preparer test administered by the IRS between November 2011 and January 2013.
2. State-based return preparer program participants currently with testing requirements: Return preparers who are active registrants of the Oregon Board of Tax Practitioners, California Tax Education Council, and/or Maryland State Board of Individual Tax Preparers.
3. SEE Part I Test-Passers: Tax practitioners who have passed the Special Enrollment Exam Part I within the past two years.
4. VITA volunteers: Quality reviewers, instructors, and return preparers.
5. Other accredited tax-focused credential holders: The Accreditation Council for Accountancy and Taxation

Accredited Business Accountant/Advisor (ABA) and Accredited Tax Preparer (ATP) programs.

6. All others need 18 hours annually.

For those who are required to obtain 15 hours, the courses must be in the following categories:

- 10 hours – Federal Tax Law
- 3 hours – Federal Tax Law Updates
- 2 hours – Ethics

For those who are required to obtain 18 hours, the courses must be in the following categories:

- 10 hours – Federal Tax Law
- 6 hours – Annual Federal Tax Refresher
- 2 hours – Ethics

**Unenrolled Tax Return Preparers**

An unenrolled return preparer is an individual other than an attorney, CPA, enrolled agent, enrolled retirement plan agent, or enrolled actuary who prepares and signs a taxpayer's return as the paid preparer, or who prepares a return but is not required (by the instructions to the return or regulations) to sign the return.

Unenrolled return preparers may represent taxpayers only before revenue agents, customer service representatives, or similar officers and employees of the Internal Revenue Service (including the Taxpayer Advocate Service) and only during an examination of the tax returns they prepared and signed prior to December 31, 2015.

- Unenrolled return preparers may not represent taxpayers before appeals officers, revenue officers, counsel or similar officers or employees of the Internal Revenue Service or the Department of the Treasury.
- Unenrolled return preparers may not execute closing agreements, extend the statutory period for tax assessments or collection of tax, execute waivers, or sign any document on behalf of a taxpayer.

If an unenrolled return preparer does not meet the requirements for limited representation, taxpayers may authorize the unenrolled return preparer to inspect and/or request the tax information by filing Form 8821. Completing Form 8821 will not authorize the unenrolled return preparer to represent the taxpayer before the IRS.

Practice denied. Any individual engaged in limited practice before the IRS who is involved in disreputable conduct is subject to disciplinary action.

Disreputable conduct includes, but is not limited to, the list of items under Incompetence and Disreputable Conduct shown, later, under What Are the Rules of Practice.

## Other Individuals Who May Serve as Representatives

Because of their special relationship with a taxpayer, the following individuals may represent the specified taxpayers before the IRS, provided they present satisfactory identification and, except in the case of an individual described in (1) below, proof of authority to represent the taxpayer.

- **An individual.** An individual can represent himself or herself before the IRS and does not have to file a written declaration of qualification and authority.
- **A family member.** An individual can represent members of his or her immediate family. Immediate family includes a spouse, child, parent, brother, or sister of the individual.
- **An officer.** A bona fide officer of a corporation (including a parent, subsidiary, or other affiliated corporation), association, or organized group can represent the corporation, association, or organized group. An officer of a governmental unit, agency, or authority, during his or her official duties, can represent the governmental unit, agency, or authority before the IRS.
- **A partner.** A general partner can represent the partnership before the IRS.
- **An employee.** A regular full-time employee can represent his or her employer. An employer can be, but is not limited to, an individual, partnership, corporation (including a parent, subsidiary, or other affiliated corporation), association, trust,

receivership, guardianship, estate, organized group, governmental unit, agency, or authority.

- **A fiduciary.** A fiduciary (trustee, executor, personal representative, administrator, receiver, or guardian) stands in the position of a taxpayer and acts as the taxpayer, not as a representative. See Fiduciary under When Is a Power of Attorney Not Required Gross Income Test.

## Representation Outside the United States

Any individual may represent an individual or entity, who is outside the United States, before personnel of the IRS when such representation also occurs outside the United States.

## Who May Not Practice Before the IRS?

In general, individuals who are not eligible, or who have lost the privilege because of certain actions, may not practice before the IRS. If an individual loses eligibility to practice, the IRS will not recognize a power of attorney that names the individual as a representative.

Corporations, associations, partnerships, and other persons that are not individuals. These organizations (or persons) are not eligible to practice before the IRS.

### Loss of Eligibility

Generally, individuals lose their eligibility to practice before the IRS in the following ways:

- Not meeting the requirements for renewal of enrollment (such as continuing professional education).
- Requesting as an enrolled agent to be placed in inactive retirement status.
- Being suspended or disbarred, or determined ineligible for practice, by the Office of Professional Responsibility for violating the regulations contained in Circular 230 or the standards in Revenue Procedure 81-38.

- Losing their state license to practice as an attorney or a certified public accountant, irrespective of the basis for the license revocation.
- Failure to meet requirements. Enrolled individuals and AFSP Record of Completion holders who fail to comply with the requirements for eligibility for renewal will be notified by the IRS. The notice will explain the reason for ineligibility and provide the individual with a time-sensitive opportunity to furnish information for reconsideration.
  - Inactive roster. An enrolled individual will be placed on the roster of inactive enrolled individuals for a period of three years, if he or she:
  - Fails to respond timely to the notice of noncompliance with the renewal requirements,
  - Fails to file timely the application for renewal or does not satisfy the requirements for renewal.
- The enrolled individual must file an application for renewal within 3 years and satisfy all requirements for renewal after being placed in inactive status. Otherwise, at the conclusion of the next renewal cycle, he or she will be removed from the roster and the enrollment status will be terminated.
- Inactive retirement status. Enrolled individuals who request to be placed in an inactive retirement status will be ineligible to practice before the IRS. They must continue to adhere to all renewal requirements. They can be reinstated to active enrollment status by filing an application for renewal and providing evidence that they have completed the required continuing professional education hours for the enrollment cycle.


## Actions That Are Not Practice Before the IRS

There are three main items that are not considered "practice before the IRS":

1. Appearing as a witness for a taxpayer. Individuals can appear as a witness but not advocate for the taxpayer.
2. Preparing a tax return. Preparing and signing tax returns is not practice before the IRS.

3. Representation of taxpayers before the US Tax court which has its own rules of practice.

**Conduct That Is Considered Disreputable**

Individuals subject to Circular 230 may be disbarred or suspended from practice before the IRS, or censured, for incompetence or disreputable conduct. A monetary penalty may also be imposed, in addition to any other discipline, on both individuals and their firms. The following list contains examples of conduct that is considered disreputable. Further examples are shown in Circular 230, Sec. 10.51(a).

- Being convicted of any criminal offense under the internal revenue laws or of any offense involving dishonesty or breach of trust.
- Knowingly giving false or misleading information in connection with federal tax matters or participating in such activity.
- Soliciting employment by prohibited means as discussed in section 10.30 of Circular 230.
- Willfully failing to file a federal tax return, evading or attempting to evade any federal tax or payment, or participating in such actions.
- Misappropriating, or failing to properly and promptly remit, funds received from clients for payment of taxes or other obligations due the United States.
- Directly or indirectly attempting to influence the official action of IRS employees using threats, false accusations, duress, or coercion, or by offering gifts, favors, or any special inducements.
- Being disbarred or suspended from practice as an attorney, CPA, public accountant, or actuary, by the District of Columbia or any U.S. state, possession, territory, commonwealth, or any federal court, or any federal agency, body, or board.
- Knowingly aiding and abetting another person to practice before the IRS during a period of suspension, disbarment, or ineligibility of that other person.

- Using abusive language, making false accusations or statements knowing them to be false, circulating or publishing malicious or libelous matter, or engaging in any contemptuous conduct in connection with practice before the IRS.
- Giving a false opinion knowingly, recklessly, or through gross incompetence; or engaging in a pattern of providing incompetent opinions on questions arising under the federal tax laws.

**Practitioner Priority Service® (PPS).**

The Practitioner Priority Service® is a nationwide, toll-free hotline that provides professional support to practitioners with account-related questions. The toll-free number for this service is 1-866-860-4259.

**What Are the Rules of Practice?**

The rules governing practice before the IRS are published in the Code of Federal Regulations at and released digitally as Treasury Department Circular No. 230.

The regulations can be accessed at

IRS.gov/Tax-Professionals/Circular-230-TaxProfessionals

An attorney, CPA, enrolled agent, enrolled retirement plan agent, or enrolled actuary authorized to practice before the IRS (referred to hereafter as a practitioner) and an appraiser has the duty to perform certain acts and is restricted from performing other acts.

In addition, a practitioner cannot engage in disreputable conduct.

Any practitioner who does not comply with the rules of practice or who engages in incompetent or disreputable conduct is subject to disciplinary action.

Also, unenrolled return preparers must comply with the rules of practice and conduct to exercise the privilege of limited practice before the IRS. There are two specific sets of rules that apply, both are contained in Circular 230:

1. Duties and restrictions relating to practice (Subpart B of Cir. 230), and
2. Conduct considered to exhibit incompetence or disrepute (Subpart C, Section 10.51 of Cir. 230).

## Duties and Restrictions

Individuals subject to Circular 230 must promptly submit records or information sought by a proper and lawful request from officers or employees of the IRS, except when the practitioner believes on reasonable grounds and good faith that the information is privileged.

Communications with respect to tax advice between a federally authorized tax practitioner and a taxpayer generally are confidential to the same extent that communication would be privileged if it were between a taxpayer and an attorney if the advice relates to: Noncriminal tax matters before the IRS, or Noncriminal tax proceedings brought in federal court by or against the United States.

## Communications regarding corporate tax shelters.

This protection for tax advice communications does not apply to any written communications between a federally authorized tax practitioner and any person, including a director, shareholder, officer, employee, agent, or representative of a corporation if the communication involves the promotion of the direct or indirect participation of the corporation in any tax shelter.

# POP QUIZ & ANSWER SHEET
# PRACTICE BEFORE THE IRS

POP QUIZ

Test your knowledge on Practice Before the IRS by answering the questions below. The answer sheet may be found at the end of the Pop Quiz.

**Q1: Which office is generally responsible for matters related to practitioner conduct and discipline within the IRS?**

    A. The Office of Professional Responsibility

    B. The Return Preparer Office

    C. The Taxpayer Advocate Service

    D. The Office of the Commissioner

**Q2: Which form must a recognized representative file with the IRS to be designated as the taxpayer's representative?**

    A. Form 1040

    B. Form 2848

    C. Form 8821

    D. Form 4506-T

**Q3: Who among the following is not permitted to practice before the IRS?**

    A. Attorneys

    B. Certified Public Accountants (CPAs)

    C. Enrolled Retirement Plan Agents

    D. Corporations

**Q4: Which of the following actions is not considered practice before the IRS?**

    A. Preparing and signing tax returns

    B. Representing a taxpayer at IRS hearings

    C. Providing written tax advice on federal tax matters

    D. Communicating with the IRS on behalf of a taxpayer

**Q5: What is the continuing education (CE) requirements for participants in the Annual Filing Season Program who need 18 hours of CE?**

    A. 10 hours of Federal Tax Law, 6 hours of Annual Federal Tax Refresher, 2 hours of ethics

    B. 12 hours of Federal Tax Law, 4 hours of Ethics, 2 hours of Tax Updates

    C. 15 hours of Federal Tax Law, 1 hour of Ethics, 2 hours of Tax Updates

    D. 8 hours of Federal Tax Law, 8 hours of Ethics, 2 hours of Tax Updates

**Q6: Which of the following is an example of disreputable conduct under Circular 230?**

    A. Failing to update the PTIN annually

    B. Preparing a tax return with minor errors

    C. Conviction of a criminal offense involving dishonesty

    D. Making a mistake on a client's tax return

**Q7: What must an enrolled agent in inactive status do to reinstate active enrollment?**

    A. File a new Form 1040

    B. Submit Form W-7

    C. Provide evidence of completed continuing professional education hours and file an application for renewal

    D. Pay a reinstatement fee and complete a new enrollment test

**Q8: What protection does the confidentiality of tax advice communications provide under Circular 230?**

A. Absolute immunity from IRS inquiries

B. Confidentiality to the same extent as communications between a taxpayer and an attorney

C. Complete exemption from submitting any records to the IRS

D. Permanent confidentiality of all tax advice communications

**Q9: What is required for a tax preparer to participate in the Annual Filing Season Program?**

A. Obtaining a PTIN and completing the necessary continuing education

B. Filing a separate tax return

C. Being a CPA or an attorney

D. Preparing a minimum of 100 tax returns annually

**Q10: Which group of individuals can represent a taxpayer before the IRS without being listed in the Directory of Federal Tax Return Preparers with Credentials and Select Qualifications?**

A. Attorneys

B. Family members

C. Enrolled Agents

D. CPAs

# Answer Sheet
## Practice Before The IRS

### Question 1:

- **Answer:** A. The Office of Professional Responsibility

- **Explanation:** The Office of Professional Responsibility handles practitioner conduct and discipline, including disciplinary proceedings and sanctions.

### Question 2:

- **Answer:** B. Form 2848

- **Explanation:** Form 2848 is used to designate a representative and file a written declaration with the IRS stating the representative's authorization and qualification.

### Question 3:

- **Answer:** D. Corporations

- **Explanation:** Corporations, associations, partnerships, and other non-individual entities are not eligible to practice before the IRS.

## Question 4:

- **Answer:** A. Preparing and signing tax returns

- **Explanation:** Preparing and signing tax returns is not considered practice before the IRS according to Circular 230.

## Question 5:

- **Answer:** A. 10 hours of Federal Tax Law, 6 hours of Annual Federal Tax Refresher, 2 hours of ethics

- **Explanation:** Participants in the Annual Filing Season Program who need 18 hours of CE must complete 10 hours of Federal Tax Law, 6 hours of Annual Federal Tax Refresher, and 2 hours of Ethics.

## Question 6:

- **Answer:** C. Conviction of a criminal offense involving dishonesty

- **Explanation:** Being convicted of any criminal offense involving dishonesty or breach of trust is considered disreputable conduct under Circular 230.

## Question 7:

- **Answer:** C. Provide evidence of completed continuing professional education hours and file an application for renewal

- **Explanation:** An enrolled agent in inactive status must file an application for renewal and provide evidence of completed continuing professional education hours to reinstate active enrollment.

## Question 8:

- **Answer:** B. Confidentiality to the same extent as communications between a taxpayer and an attorney

- **Explanation:** Communications with respect to tax advice between a federally authorized tax practitioner and a taxpayer are generally confidential to the same extent that they would be between a taxpayer and an attorney, as long as the advice relates to noncriminal tax matters before the IRS or noncriminal tax proceedings brought in federal court by or against the United States.

## Question 9:

- **Answer:** A. Obtaining a PTIN and completing the necessary continuing education

- **Explanation:** To participate in the Annual Filing Season Program, a tax preparer must obtain a Preparer Tax Identification Number (PTIN) and complete the necessary continuing education.

## Question 10:

- **Answer:** B. Family members

- **Explanation:** Family members can represent their immediate family before the IRS without being listed in the Directory of Federal Tax Return Preparers with Credentials and Select Qualifications.

# Requirements for Enrolled Agents

## Overview

This part contains rules governing the recognition of attorneys, certified public accountants, enrolled agents, enrolled retirement plan agents, registered tax return preparers, and other persons representing taxpayers before the Internal Revenue Service.

### Information To Be Furnished to the IRS

(1) A practitioner must, on a proper and lawful request by a duly authorized officer or employee of the Internal Revenue Service, promptly submit records or information in any matter before the Internal Revenue Service unless the practitioner believes in good faith and on reasonable grounds that the records or information are privileged.

**Example**: Lisa, an Enrolled Agent receives a proper and lawful request from an authorized IRS officer or employee for certain records or information related to a client's tax matter.

Lisa's client, Mark, is being audited by the IRS, and the auditor requests copies of specific financial statements and receipts to verify the deductions claimed on Mark's tax return. The auditor contacts Lisa and asks her to promptly submit the requested records.

In accordance with the provision stated, Lisa must comply with the request unless she has a good faith belief, supported by reasonable grounds, that the records or information are privileged. If Lisa knows that the requested documents are protected by attorney-client privilege or another recognized privilege, she may refuse to disclose them to the IRS.

However, if Lisa does not believe there are any applicable privileges or if she does not have a reasonable basis to assert privilege, she is obligated to promptly submit the requested records or information to the IRS. Failure to comply with the lawful request without a valid reason could result in penalties or other consequences for Lisa as a practitioner.

(2) Where the requested records or information are not in the possession of, or subject to the control of, the practitioner or the practitioner's client, the practitioner must promptly notify the requesting Internal Revenue Service officer or employee and the practitioner must provide any information that the practitioner has regarding the identity of any person who the practitioner believes may have possession or control of the requested records or information.

The practitioner must make reasonable inquiry of his or her client regarding the identity of any person who may have possession or control of the requested records or information, but the practitioner is not required to make inquiry of any other person or independently verify any information provided by the practitioner's client regarding the identity of such persons.

(3) When a proper and lawful request is made by a duly authorized officer or employee of the Internal Revenue Service, concerning an inquiry into an alleged violation of the regulations in this part, a practitioner must provide any information the practitioner has concerning the alleged violation and testify regarding this information in any proceeding instituted under this part, unless the practitioner believes in good faith and on reasonable grounds that the information is privileged.

(b) Interference with a proper and lawful request for records or information. A practitioner may not interfere, or attempt to interfere, with any proper and lawful effort by the Internal Revenue Service, its officers or employees, to obtain any record or information unless the practitioner believes in good faith and on reasonable grounds that the record or information is privileged.

**For example:** An Internal Revenue Agent showed up at Agnes EA firm. The Agent requested all documents for one of her business clients. After verifying the agent, Agnes gives all documents requested after making copies for herself to the RA. Agnes also calls the client who has the remainder of the documents, and she informs the client that all other documents need to be given to the RA. She also asks the client if there is anyone who might have further documents. Agnes has fulfilled her requirements.

## Omission or error on return, document, or affidavit

A practitioner who, having been retained by a client with respect to a matter administered by the Internal Revenue Service, knows that the client has not complied with the revenue laws of the United States or has made an error in or omission from any return, document, affidavit, or other paper which the client submitted or executed under the revenue laws of the United States, must advise the client promptly of the fact of such noncompliance, error, or omission. The practitioner must advise the client of the consequences as provided under the Code and regulations of such noncompliance, error, or omission.

**For Example:** Rachel, an Enrolled Agent discovered that her client Mario omitted pertinent information on his tax return. She notified Mario immediately of the omittance and informed him of the requirements to amend the return and the possible penalties for not making the correction. Rachel can offer to amend the return for her going rate, but she is not obligated to make the correction or to notify the IRS.

## Rules for Employing or Accepting Assistance from Disbarred/Suspended Persons

A practitioner may not, knowingly and directly or indirectly:

(a) Accept assistance from or assist any person who is under disbarment or suspension from practice before the Internal Revenue Service if the assistance relates to a matter or matters constituting practice before the Internal Revenue Service.

(b) Accept assistance from any former government employee where the provisions of § 10.25 or any Federal law would be violated.

## Rules for Employing or Accepting Assistance from Former IRS Employees

(1) No former Government employee may, subsequent to Government employment, represent anyone in any matter administered by the Internal Revenue Service if the representation would violate 18 U.S.C. 207 or any other laws of the United States.

(2) No former Government employee who personally and substantially participated in a particular matter involving specific parties may, subsequent to Government employment, represent or knowingly assist, in that particular matter, any person who is or was a specific party to that particular matter.

(3) A former Government employee who within a period of one year prior to the termination of Government employment had official responsibility for a particular matter involving specific parties may not, within two years after Government employment is ended, represent in that particular matter any person who is or was a specific party to that  particular matter.

## Rules for Fee Information § 10.27 Fees.

A practitioner may not charge an unconscionable fee in connection with any matter before the Internal Revenue Service.

(b) Contingent fees — (1) Except as provided in paragraphs (b)(2), (3), and (4) of this section, a practitioner may not charge a contingent fee for services rendered in connection with any matter before the Internal Revenue Service.

(2) A practitioner may charge a contingent fee for  services rendered in connection with the Service's  examination of, or challenge to — (i) An original tax  return; or (ii) An amended return or claim for refund  or credit where the amended return or claim for  refund or credit was filed within 120 days of the taxpayer receiving a written notice of the examination  of, or a written challenge to the original tax return.

(3) A practitioner may charge a contingent fee for services rendered in connection with a claim for credit or refund filed solely in connection with the determination of statutory interest or penalties assessed by the Internal Revenue Service.

(4) A practitioner may charge a contingent fee for services rendered in connection with any judicial proceeding arising under the Internal Revenue Code.

**Definitions.** For purposes of this section — (1) Contingent fee is any fee that is based, in whole or in part, on whether or not a position taken on a tax return or other filing avoids challenge by the Internal Revenue Service or is sustained either by the Internal Revenue Service or in litigation. A contingent fee includes a fee that is based on a percentage of the refund reported on a return, that is based on a percentage of the taxes saved, or that otherwise depends on the specific result attained. A contingent fee also includes any fee arrangement in which the practitioner will reimburse the client for all or a portion of the client's fee in the event

**For example:** John charges a percentage of the tax return for all of his clients. The bigger he is able to get the refund the more his fee will be. John is in violation of circular 230 by charging these contingent fees. The appropriate way to charge fees will be to charge based on the complexity of the tax return on a per form basis.

**Example 2:** Jordan charges a contingent fee to his client Allie for the audit of her business tax return that was an original return for tax year. Jordan is compliant with circular 230 because practitioners can charge contingent fees in matters of audits, examinations or before tax court.

**Rules for restrictions on advertising, solicitation and fee information**

(1) A practitioner may not, with respect to any Internal Revenue Service matter, in any way use or participate in the use of any form of public communication or private solicitation containing a false, fraudulent, or coercive statement or claim, or a misleading or deceptive statement or claim.

Enrolled agents, enrolled retirement plan agents, or registered tax return preparers, in describing their professional designation, may not utilize the term "certified" or imply an employer/employee relationship with the Internal Revenue Service.

Examples of acceptable descriptions for enrolled agents are

1. "enrolled to represent taxpayers before the Internal Revenue Service,"

2. "enrolled to practice before the Internal Revenue Service," and

3. "admitted to practice before the Internal Revenue Service."

Similarly, examples of acceptable descriptions for enrolled retirement plan agents are "enrolled to represent taxpayers before the Internal Revenue Service as a retirement plan agent" and "enrolled to practice before the Internal Revenue Service as a retirement plan agent."

An example of an acceptable description for registered tax return preparers is "designated as a registered tax return preparer by the Internal Revenue Service."

**For example:** Thomas a newly licensed Enrolled Agent advertises on his Instagram bio the following:

"Certified by the IRS to help tax and business clients resolve their tax debt, click the link below to access my free e-book"

This will be in direct violation of circular 230 advertising standards. The allowed way for Thomas to advertise would be to replace "Certified by the IRS" to "Enrolled to practice before the IRS"

(2) A practitioner may not make, directly or indirectly, an uninvited written or oral solicitation of employment in matters related to the Internal Revenue Service if the solicitation violates Federal or State law or other applicable rule, e.g., attorneys are precluded from making a solicitation that is prohibited by conduct rules applicable to all attorneys in their State(s) of licensure.

Any lawful solicitation made by or on behalf of a practitioner eligible to practice before the Internal Revenue Service must, nevertheless, clearly identify the solicitation as such and, if applicable, identify the source of the information used in choosing the recipient.

**For example:** You need to hire more Enrolled Agents for your firm because business is booming, so you pull the list of Enrolled Agents from IRS.gov and start to email those Ea.'s uninvited employment opportunities. This would be in violation of circular 230.

## Fee information

A practitioner may publish the availability of a written schedule of fees and disseminate the following fee information —

(A) Fixed fees for specific routine services.

(B) Hourly rates.

(C) Range of fees for particular services.

(D) Fee charged for an initial consultation.

Any statement of fee information concerning matters in which costs may be incurred must include a statement disclosing whether clients will be responsible for such costs.

A practitioner may charge no more than the rate(s) for at least 30 calendar days after the last date on which the schedule of fees was published.

**For example:** You published to your Facebook page that you charge $150 for 1040 tax preparation on January 1. You must keep this rate for 30 days, until January 31st.

## Communication of fee information.

Fee information may be communicated in professional lists, telephone directories, print media, mailings, and electronic mail, facsimile, hand delivered flyers, radio, television, and any other method.

The method chosen, however, must not cause the communication to become untruthful, deceptive, or otherwise in violation of this part.

A practitioner may not persist in attempting to contact a prospective client if the prospective client has made it known to the practitioner that he or she does not desire to be solicited. In the case of radio and television broadcasting, the broadcast must be recorded, and the practitioner must retain a recording of the actual transmission.

In the case of direct mail and e-commerce communications, the practitioner must retain a copy of the actual communication, along with a list or other description of persons to whom the communication was mailed or otherwise distributed. The copy must be retained by the practitioner for a period of at least 36 months from the date of the last transmission or use.

## Diligence As to Accuracy

A practitioner must exercise due diligence —

(1) In preparing or assisting in the preparation of, approving, and filing tax returns, documents, affidavits, and other papers relating to Internal Revenue Service matters.

(2) In determining the correctness of oral or written representations made by the practitioner to the Department of the Treasury; and

(3) In determining the correctness of oral or written representations made by the practitioner to clients with reference to any matter administered by the Internal Revenue Service.

## Reliance On Others

A practitioner will be presumed to have exercised due diligence if the practitioner relies on the work product of another person and the practitioner used reasonable care in engaging, supervising, training, and evaluating the person, taking proper account of the nature of the relationship between the practitioner and the person.

## Conflict of Interest

Except as provided by paragraph (b) of this section, a practitioner shall not represent a client before the Internal Revenue Service if the representation involves a conflict of interest.

A conflict of interest exists if —

(1) The representation of one client will be directly averse to another client: or

(2) There is a significant risk that the representation of one or more clients will be materially limited by the practitioner's responsibilities to another client, a former client or a third person, or by a personal interest of the practitioner.

The practitioner may represent a client if —

(1) The practitioner reasonably believes that the practitioner will be able to provide competent and diligent representation to each affected client.

(2) The representation is not prohibited by law; and each affected client waives the conflict of interest and gives informed consent, confirmed in writing by each affected client, at the time the existence of the conflict of interest is known by the practitioner. The confirmation may be made within a reasonable period of time after the informed consent but in no event later than 30 days.

Copies of the written consents must be retained by the practitioner for at least 36 months from the **date of the conclusion of the representation** of the affected clients, and the written consents must be provided to any officer or employee of the Internal Revenue Service on request.

**For example:** You are an EA that is representing a now divorced husband and wife regarding the same tax debt for the same tax years. This would be a conflict of interest because you may not be able to represent both to the highest ability. You may decline representing both and refer them both to different EA's or if you truly believe that you can represent both then you must immediately notify them both of the conflict of interest and get in writing their consent. If the representation ended December 1. You must keep the consent on file for 36 months of 3 years from December 1.

## Rules for Refund Check Negotiation

A practitioner may not endorse or otherwise negotiate any check (including directing or accepting payment by any means, electronic or otherwise, into an account owned or controlled by the practitioner or any firm or other entity with whom the practitioner is associated) issued to a client by the government in respect of a federal tax liability.

**For example:** A client asks you to deposit their refund check into your account because they don't have a bank account and to take your fee and give them the remaining amount. You cannot and should not do this. Even if the client asks. They should ask a family member or go to a check-cashing store.

## Requirements for Written Advice

A practitioner may give written advice (including by means of electronic communication) concerning one or more Federal tax matters.

The practitioner must—

- Base the written advice on reasonable factual and legal assumptions (including assumptions as to future events).
- Reasonably consider all relevant facts and circumstances that the practitioner knows or reasonably should know.
- Use reasonable efforts to identify and ascertain the facts relevant to written advice on each Federal tax matter.

- Not rely upon representations, statements, findings, or agreements (including projections, financial forecasts, or appraisals) of the taxpayer or any other person if reliance on them would be unreasonable.
- Relate applicable law and authorities to facts; and
- Not, in evaluating a federal tax matter, take into account the possibility that a tax return will not be audited or that a matter will not be raised on audit.

Reliance on representations, statements, findings, or agreements is unreasonable if the practitioner knows or reasonably should know that one or more representations or assumptions on which any representation is based are incorrect, incomplete, or inconsistent.

## Reliance on advice from others

A practitioner may only rely on the advice of another person if the advice was reasonable, and the reliance is in good faith considering all the facts and circumstances.

Reliance is not reasonable when—

(1) The practitioner knows or reasonably should know that the opinion of the other person should not be relied on.

(2) The practitioner knows or reasonably should know that the other person is not competent or lacks the necessary qualifications to provide the advice; or

(3) The practitioner knows or reasonably should know that the other person has a conflict of interest in violation of the rules described in this part.

## Continuing Education Requirements

Enrolled agents must obtain 72 hours of continuing education every three years. Remember this number of 72.

A minimum of 16 hours must be earned per year, two of which must be on ethics. Enrolled agents must use an IRS approved CE provider.

Preparers must retain the following records for four years:

- The name of the CE Provider organization.
- The location of the program.
- The title of the program, approval number received for the program, and copy of the program content.
- Written outlines, course syllabi, textbook, and/or electronic materials provided or required for the program.
- The date(s) attended.
- The credit hours claimed.
- The name(s) of the instructor(s), discussion leader(s), or speaker(s), if appropriate; and
- The certificate of completion and/or signed statement of the hours of attendance obtained from the continuing education provider

Enrolled Agents should look at the public listing for approved providers. Approved providers may also show the "IRS Approved Continuing Education Provider" logo. In addition, all providers are issued a Provider Number from the IRS.

### Prompt Disposition of Pending Matters

A practitioner may not unreasonably delay the prompt disposition of any matter before the Internal Revenue Service.

### Rules for returning a client's records and documents

A practitioner must, at the request of a client, promptly return any and all records of the client that are necessary for the client to comply with his or her federal tax obligations.

The practitioner may retain copies of the records returned to a client.

The existence of a dispute over fees generally does not relieve the practitioner of his or her responsibility under this section.

Nevertheless, if applicable state law allows or permits the retention of a client's records by a practitioner in the case of a dispute over fees for services rendered, the practitioner need only return those records that must be attached to the taxpayer's return.

The practitioner, however, must provide the client with reasonable access to review and copy any additional records of the client retained by the practitioner under state law that are necessary for the client to comply with his or her federal tax obligations.

Records of the client include all documents or written, or electronic materials provided to the practitioner, or obtained by the practitioner in the course of the practitioner's representation of the client, that preexisted the retention of the practitioner by the client.

The term also includes materials that were prepared by the client or a third party (not including an employee or agent of the practitioner) at any time and provided to the practitioner with respect to the subject matter of the representation.

The term also includes any return, claim for refund, schedule, affidavit, appraisal or any other document prepared by the practitioner, or his or her employee or agent, that was presented to the client with respect to a prior representation if such document is necessary for the taxpayer to comply with his or her current Federal tax obligations.

The term does not include any return, claim for refund, schedule, affidavit, appraisal or any other document prepared by the practitioner or the practitioner's firm, employees or agents if the practitioner is withholding such document pending the client's performance of its contractual obligation to pay fees with respect to such document.

**For example:** You prepared a client's tax return, and they didn't like the results. They decide not to pay you and to go somewhere else. You are required by circular 230 to give them all source documents they gave you such as their 1099s, w2s, etc to prepare their tax returns. You do not have to give them the tax return you completed as that is your work product that they didn't pay for.

## Preparer Tax Identification Requirements (PTIN)

All enrolled agents must renew their preparer tax identification number as prescribed by forms, instructions, or other appropriate guidance.

Any individual who for compensation prepares or assists with the preparation of all or substantially all of a tax return or claim for refund must have a preparer tax identification number

# Pop Quiz & Answer Sheet
# Requirements for Enrolled Agents

## POP QUIZ

Test your knowledge on *Requirements for Enrolled Agents* by answering the questions below. The answer sheet may be found at the end of the Pop Quiz.

**Q1: What is the responsibility of the Office of Professional Responsibility?**

    A. Issuing PTINs and administering competency testing
    B. Handling practitioner conduct and discipline
    C. Providing taxpayer assistance
    D. Managing tax return processing

**Q2: Under what condition can a practitioner refuse to submit requested records or information to the IRS?**

    A. If the practitioner believes the request is too burdensome
    B. If the practitioner believes in good faith and on reasonable grounds that the records or information are privileged
    C. If the practitioner thinks the records are not relevant
    D. If the practitioner has not yet obtained the client's permission

**Q3: What must a practitioner do if requested records or information are not in their possession or control?**

    A. Inform the IRS that they do not have the records
    B. Notify the IRS officer and provide any information regarding the identity of the person who may have possession or control of the records
    C. Ignore the request
    D. Ask the IRS for more time to find the records

**Q4: Which of the following is considered disreputable conduct under Circular 230?**

    A. Preparing a tax return with minor errors
    B. Soliciting clients through social media
    C. Misappropriating client funds
    D. Offering tax advice to clients


**Q5: How long must enrolled agents keep records of their continuing education?**

    A. 1 year
    B. 2 years
    C. 3 years
    D. 4 years


**Q6: What is the required minimum number of continuing education hours enrolled agents must complete each year?**

    A. 10 hours
    B. 12 hours
    C. 16 hours
    D. 18 hours


**Q7: Which of the following is not allowed under Circular 230 regarding fees?**

    A. Charging an hourly rate for tax preparation services
    B. Charging a contingent fee for an original tax return
    C. Charging a fixed fee for specific routine services
    D. Charging a fee based on the complexity of the tax return

**Q8: How should a practitioner advertise their services to comply with Circular 230?**

A. By stating they are "certified by the IRS"
B. By stating they are "enrolled to practice before the IRS"
C. By stating they are "approved by the IRS"
D. By stating they are "licensed by the IRS"

**Q9: What should a practitioner do if they discover their client has made an error or omission on a tax return?**

A. Ignore the error and proceed
B. Notify the IRS immediately
C. Advise the client promptly of the error and the consequences
D. Correct the error without informing the client

**Q10: Which of the following records must a practitioner return to a client upon request?**

A. The practitioner's work product
B. Source documents provided by the client
C. Copies of the client's tax returns prepared by the practitioner
D. The practitioner's notes

# Answer Sheet
# Requirements for Enrolled Agents

## Question 1:

- **Answer:** B. Handling practitioner conduct and discipline

- **Explanation:** The Office of Professional Responsibility is responsible for matters related to practitioner conduct and discipline, including disciplinary proceedings and sanctions.

## Question 2:

- **Answer:** B. If the practitioner believes in good faith and on reasonable grounds that the records or information are privileged

- **Explanation:** A practitioner must promptly submit requested records or information unless they believe in good faith and on reasonable grounds that the records or information are privileged.

## Question 3:

- **Answer:** B. Notify the IRS officer and provide any information regarding the identity of the person who may have possession or control of the records

- **Explanation:** The practitioner must notify the IRS officer and provide any information they have regarding the identity of any person who may have possession or control of the requested records.

## Question 4:

- **Answer:** C. Misappropriating client funds

- **Explanation:** Misappropriating, or failing to properly and promptly remit, funds received from clients for payment of taxes or other obligations due to the United States is considered disreputable conduct.


## Question 5:

- **Answer:** D. 4 years

- **Explanation:** Enrolled agents must retain records of their continuing education for four years.


## Question 6:

- **Answer:** C. 16 hours

- **Explanation:** Enrolled agents must obtain a minimum of 16 hours of continuing education each year, two of which must be on ethics.


## Question 7:

- **Answer:** B. Charging a contingent fee for an original tax return

- **Explanation:** Practitioners may not charge a contingent fee for services rendered in connection with any matter before the IRS, except in specific cases such as audits or judicial proceedings.

# Question 8:

- **Answer:** B. By stating they are "enrolled to practice before the IRS"

- **Explanation:** Practitioners must use terms like "enrolled to practice before the IRS" and avoid using terms like "certified by the IRS" which could be misleading.

# Question 9:

- **Answer:** C. Advise the client promptly of the error and the consequences

- **Explanation:** The practitioner must advise the client promptly of the error or omission and the consequences under the Code and regulations.

# Question 10:

- **Answer:** B. Source documents provided by the client

- **Explanation:** The practitioner must return any and all records of the client necessary for the client to comply with their federal tax obligations, including source documents provided by the client.

# Sanctionable Acts

## Overview

This part prescribes the sanctions that practitioners will be subject to for violating the regulations.

## Badges of Fraud

There is no federal statute that definitively lists each badge of fraud. These red flags have been cultivated after years of court decisions. Some common badges include (but are not limited to):

- Understatement or complete omission of income
- Keeping two sets of books (or other accounting irregularities)
- Improper deductions or credits
- Lying to IRS agents, destroying records, or engaging in other deceptive activities
- Manipulating tax returns or documents to conceal illegal activities
- Not keeping adequate records
- Failing to file required tax returns
- Consistently engaging in underreporting or omission of taxable income

## Authority to censure, suspend, or disbar.

The Secretary of the Treasury, or delegate, after notice and an opportunity for a proceeding, may censure, suspend, or disbar any practitioner from practice before the Internal Revenue Service if the practitioner is shown to be incompetent or disreputable, fails to comply with any regulation in this part or with intent to defraud, willfully and knowingly misleads or threatens a client or prospective client.

Censure is a public reprimand.

**Authority to impose monetary penalty**

The Secretary of the Treasury, or delegate, after notice and an opportunity for a proceeding, may impose a monetary penalty on any practitioner who engages in conduct subject to sanction.

If the practitioner described was acting on behalf of an employer or any firm or other entity in connection with the conduct giving rise to the penalty, the Secretary of the Treasury, or delegate, may impose a monetary penalty on the employer, firm, or entity if it knew, or reasonably should have known of such conduct.

**Amount of penalty**

The amount of the penalty shall not exceed the gross income derived (or to be derived) from the conduct giving rise to the penalty.

**Coordination with other sanctions**

Any monetary penalty imposed on a practitioner may be in addition to or in lieu of any suspension, disbarment or censure and may be in addition to a penalty imposed on an employer, firm or other entity.

Any monetary penalty imposed on an employer, firm or other entity may be in addition to or in lieu of penalties imposed.

**Authority to accept a practitioner's consent to sanction**

The Internal Revenue Service may accept a practitioner's offer of consent to be sanctioned under §10.50 in lieu of instituting or continuing a proceeding under §10.60(a).

**Sanctions to be imposed**

The sanctions imposed by this section shall take into account all relevant facts and circumstances.

## Incompetence and Disreputable Conduct

Incompetence and disreputable conduct for which a practitioner may be sanctioned under §10.50 includes, but is not limited to —

1. Conviction of any criminal offense under the Federal tax laws.
2. Conviction of any criminal offense involving dishonesty or breach of trust.
3. Conviction of any felony under Federal or State law for which the conduct involved renders the practitioner unfit to practice before the Internal Revenue Service.
4. Giving false or misleading information, or participating in any way in the giving of false or misleading information to the Department of the Treasury or any officer or employee thereof, or to any tribunal authorized to pass upon Federal tax matters, in connection with any matter pending or likely to be pending before them, knowing the information to be false or misleading.
5. Solicitation of employment as prohibited under §10.30, the use of false or misleading representations with intent to deceive a client or prospective client in order to procure employment or intimating that the practitioner is able improperly to obtain special consideration or action from the Internal Revenue Service or any officer or employee thereof.
6. Willfully failing to make a federal tax return in violation of the Federal tax laws, or willfully evading, attempting to evade, or participating in any way in evading or attempting to evade any assessment or payment of any Federal tax.
7. Willfully assisting, counseling, encouraging a client or prospective client in violating, or suggesting to a client or prospective client to violate, any Federal tax law, or knowingly counseling or suggesting to a client or prospective client an illegal plan to evade Federal taxes or payment thereof.
8. Misappropriation of, or failure properly or promptly to remit, funds received from a client for the purpose of payment of taxes or other obligations due the United States.
9. Directly or indirectly attempting to influence, or offering or agreeing to attempt to influence, the official action of any

officer or employee of the Internal Revenue Service by the use of threats, false accusations, duress or coercion, by the offer of any special inducement or promise of an advantage or by the bestowing of any gift, favor or thing of value.

10. Disbarment or suspension from practice as an attorney, certified public accountant, public accountant, or actuary by any duly constituted authority of any State, territory, or possession of the United States, including a Commonwealth, or the District of Columbia, any Federal court of record or any Federal agency, body or board.

11. Knowingly aiding and abetting another person to practice before the Internal Revenue Service during a period of suspension, disbarment or ineligibility of such other person.

12. Contemptuous conduct in connection with practice before the Internal Revenue Service, including the use of abusive language, making false accusations or statements, knowing them to be false, or circulating or publishing malicious or libelous matter.

13. Giving a false opinion, knowingly, recklessly, or through gross incompetence, including an opinion which is intentionally or recklessly misleading, or engaging in a pattern of providing incompetent opinions on questions arising under the Federal tax laws. False opinions include those which reflect or result from a knowing misstatement of fact or law, from an assertion of a position known to be unwarranted under existing law, from counseling or assisting in conduct known to be illegal or fraudulent, from concealing matters required by law to be revealed, or from consciously disregarding information indicating that material facts expressed in the opinion or offering material are false or misleading.

14. A pattern of conduct is a factor that will be taken into account in determining whether a practitioner acted knowingly, recklessly, or through gross incompetence. Gross incompetence includes conduct that reflects gross indifference, preparation which is grossly inadequate under the circumstances, and a consistent failure to perform obligations to the client.

15. Willfully failing to sign a tax return prepared by the practitioner when the practitioner's signature is required by

Federal tax laws unless the failure is due to reasonable cause and not due to willful neglect.

16. Willfully disclosing or otherwise using a tax return or tax return information in a manner not authorized by the Internal Revenue Code, contrary to the order of a court of competent jurisdiction, or contrary to the order of an administrative law judge in a proceeding instituted under §10.60.

17. Willfully failing to file on magnetic or other electronic media a tax return prepared by the practitioner when the practitioner is required to do so by the Federal tax laws unless the failure is due to reasonable cause and not due to willful neglect.

18. Willfully preparing all or substantially all of, or signing, a tax return or claim for refund when the practitioner does not possess a current or otherwise valid preparer tax identification number or other prescribed identifying number.

19. Willfully representing a taxpayer before an officer or employee of the Internal Revenue Service unless the practitioner is authorized to do so pursuant to this part.

**Violations Subject to Sanction.**

A practitioner may be sanctioned under §10.50 if the practitioner

(1) Willfully violates any of the regulations or

(2) Recklessly or through gross incompetence

**Receipt of information concerning practitioner.**

If an officer or employee of the Internal Revenue Service has reason to believe a practitioner has violated any provision, the officer or employee will promptly make a written report of the suspected violation. The report will explain the facts and reasons upon which the officer's or employee's belief rests and must be submitted to the office(s) of the Internal Revenue Service responsible for administering or enforcing this part.

# Pop Quiz & Answer Sheet
## Sanctionable Acts

## POP QUIZ

Test your knowledge on *Sanctionable Acts* by answering the questions below. The answer sheet may be found at the end of the Pop Quiz.

### Q1: Which of the following is considered a badge of fraud?

    A. Overstating expenses on a tax return
    B. Keeping accurate records for all transactions
    C. Filing tax returns on time
    D. Reporting all income accurately

### Q2: What authority does the Secretary of the Treasury have regarding practitioners who violate regulations?

    A. They can only issue a warning
    B. They can censure, suspend, or disbar the practitioner
    C. They can impose a mandatory training course
    D. They can increase the practitioner's client base

### Q3: What is the maximum amount of a monetary penalty that can be imposed on a practitioner for sanctionable conduct?

    A. $10,000
    B. Twice the practitioner's annual income
    C. The gross income derived from the conduct giving rise to the penalty
    D. $100,000

**Q4: What is an example of disreputable conduct that could lead to a practitioner being sanctioned?**

A. Preparing a tax return with minor errors
B. Willfully failing to make a federal tax return
C. Accurately reporting all client income
D. Giving honest and accurate tax advice

**Q5: Which of the following is not a valid reason for a practitioner to refuse to submit records to the IRS?**

A. The records are believed to be privileged
B. The records are not in the possession of the practitioner
C. The practitioner does not think the records are relevant
D. The records are protected by attorney-client privilege

**Q6: Under what condition can a practitioner accept assistance from a former government employee?**

A. If the assistance is related to any matter before the IRS
B. If the former government employee did not participate in the matter while employed by the government
C. If the former government employee has been out of government service for more than one year
D. If the assistance is for personal tax matters

**Q7: Which of the following actions is prohibited for practitioners regarding refund checks?**

A. Advising clients on how to deposit their refund checks
B. Negotiating a client's refund check
C. Preparing tax returns that generate refunds
D. Informing clients about the status of their refunds

**Q8: What must a practitioner do if they discover their client has made an error or omission on a tax return?**

A. Correct the error without informing the client
B. Ignore the error if it is small
C. Advise the client promptly of the error and the consequences
D. Notify the IRS immediately

**Q9: How long must practitioners retain copies of communications such as direct mail or e-commerce messages sent to clients?**

A. 1 year
B. 2 years
C. 3 years
D. 4 years

**Q10: What is required for a practitioner to resolve a conflict of interest with multiple clients?**

A. The practitioner must withdraw from representing all clients
B. Each affected client must waive the conflict of interest and give informed consent in writing
C. The practitioner must notify the IRS of the conflict
D. The practitioner can continue to represent both clients without any additional steps

# Answer Sheet
# Sanctionable Acts

## Question 1:

- **Answer:** A. Overstating expenses on a tax return

- **Explanation:** Overstating expenses on a tax return is considered a badge of fraud, as it involves improper deductions or credits, which are common indicators of fraudulent activity.

## Question 2:

- **Answer:** B. They can censure, suspend, or disbar the practitioner

- **Explanation:** The Secretary of the Treasury has the authority to censure, suspend, or disbar any practitioner from practice before the IRS if the practitioner is shown to be incompetent, disreputable, or fails to comply with regulations.

## Question 3:

- **Answer:** C. The gross income derived from the conduct giving rise to the penalty

- **Explanation:** The amount of the penalty shall not exceed the gross income derived (or to be derived) from the conduct giving rise to the penalty.

## Question 4:

- **Answer:** B. Willfully failing to make a federal tax return

- **Explanation:** Willfully failing to make a federal tax return is considered disreputable conduct and can lead to sanctions such as suspension or disbarment.

## Question 5:

- **Answer:** C. The practitioner does not think the records are relevant

- **Explanation:** A practitioner cannot refuse to submit records simply because they do not think the records are relevant. They must submit records unless they believe in good faith and on reasonable grounds that the records are privileged.

## Question 6:

- **Answer:** B. If the former government employee did not participate in the matter while employed by the government

- **Explanation:** A practitioner can accept assistance from a former government employee as long as the former employee did not personally and substantially participate in that particular matter while employed by the government.

**Question 7:**

- **Answer:** B. Negotiating a client's refund check

- **Explanation:** Practitioners may not endorse or otherwise negotiate any check issued to a client by the government in respect of a federal tax liability.

**Question 8:**

- **Answer:** C. Advise the client promptly of the error and the consequences

- **Explanation:** The practitioner must advise the client promptly of the error or omission and the consequences under the Code and regulations.

**Question 9:**

- **Answer:** C. 3 years

- **Explanation:** Practitioners must retain copies of the actual communication, along with a list or description of persons to whom the communication was sent, for at least 36 months from the date of the last transmission or use.

## Question 10:

- **Answer:** B. Each affected client must waive the conflict of interest and give informed consent in writing

- **Explanation:** The practitioner may represent a client if each affected client waives the conflict of interest and gives informed consent, confirmed in writing. The consent must be retained for at least 36 months from the conclusion of the representation.

# Rules & Penalties

## Overview

When a tax practitioner (or their employer, firm, or organization, if applicable) is found to have broken any of the rules that govern practicing before the Internal Revenue Service (IRS) or the regulations outlined in this section, the practitioner may receive a reprimand or face a formal process for penalties.

The Commissioner, or someone authorized by the Commissioner, has the authority to hold discussions with a practitioner, employer, firm, organization, or appraiser regarding allegations of misconduct, regardless of whether a formal process has been initiated.

If the discussion leads to an agreement related to an ongoing process in which the practitioner, employer, firm, organization, or appraiser is the one being investigated, the agreement can be officially recorded and considered by either party involved in the process.

### Voluntary sanction —
In lieu of a proceeding being instituted or continued, a practitioner or appraiser (or employer, firm or other entity, if applicable) may offer a consent to be sanctioned under §10.50.

Discretion; acceptance or declination. The Commissioner, or delegate, may accept or decline the offer.

When the decision is to decline the offer, the written notice of declination may state that the offer described would be accepted if it contained different terms.

The Commissioner, or delegate, has the discretion to accept or reject a revised offer submitted in response to the declination or may counteroffer and act upon any accepted counteroffer.

## Contents of Complaint

A complaint must name the respondent, provide a clear and concise description of the facts and law that constitute the basis for the proceeding, and be signed by an authorized representative of the Internal Revenue Service.

A complaint is sufficient if it fairly informs the respondent of the charges brought so that the respondent is able to prepare a defense.

## Specification of Sanction

The complaint must specify the sanction sought against the practitioner or appraiser. If the sanction sought is a suspension, the duration of the suspension sought must be specified.

## Demand for Answer

The respondent must be notified in the complaint or in a separate paper attached to the complaint of the time for answering the complaint, which may not be less than 30 days from the date of service of the complaint, the name and address of the Administrative Law Judge with whom the answer must be filed, the name and address of the person representing the Internal Revenue Service to whom a copy of the answer must be served, and that a decision by default may be rendered against the respondent in the event an answer is not filed as required.

## Failure to Deny or Answer Allegations in The Complaint

Every allegation in the complaint that is not denied in the answer is deemed admitted and will be considered proved; no further evidence in respect of such allegation need be adduced at a hearing.

**Default.** Failure to file an answer within the time prescribed (or within the time for answer as extended by the Administrative Law Judge), constitutes an admission of the allegations of the complaint and a waiver of hearing, and the Administrative Law Judge may make the decision by default without a hearing or further procedure.

**Signature.** The answer must be signed by the respondent or the respondent's authorized representative and must include a statement directly above the signature acknowledging that the statements made in the answer are true and correct and that knowing and willful false statements may be punishable.

## Accuracy-Related Penalty on Underpayments

Sec. 6662 imposes an accuracy-related penalty equal to 20% of any underpayment of federal tax resulting from certain specified taxpayer behaviors (e.g., negligence, disregard of rules or regulations, substantial understatement of income tax, and certain valuation misstatements).

The IRS can impose the accuracy-related penalty for careless, reckless, or intentional disregard of the rules or regulations, but a taxpayer may be able to avoid the penalty for taking a position on a return that is contrary to a rule or regulation if the taxpayer properly discloses the position.

## Imposition of the penalty

1. Negligence or disregard of rules or regulations.

2. Any substantial understatement of income tax.

3. Any substantial valuation misstatement.

4. Any substantial overstatement of pension liabilities.

5. Any substantial estate or gift tax valuation understatement.

6. Any disallowance of claimed tax benefits by reason of a transaction lacking economic substance.

7. Any undisclosed foreign financial asset understatement.

8. Any inconsistent estate basis.

## Reasonable-cause exception

Notwithstanding the breadth of situations where the penalty may apply, Sec. 6664(c)(1) provides an exception:

No penalty shall be imposed under section 6662 or 6663 with respect to any portion of an underpayment if it is shown that there was a reasonable cause for such portion and that the taxpayer acted in good faith with respect to such portion.

As with many areas of the law, the applicability of the exception depends on the facts and circumstances of each case. Of particular importance, of course, is the definition of "reasonable cause." The Treasury regulations provide assistance in this regard.

### Defining 'reasonable cause'

According to Regs. Sec. 1.6664-4, "the most important factor is the extent of the taxpayer's effort to assess the taxpayer's proper tax liability." Other factors the regulations state may be taken into account include:

    A. Reasonable misunderstanding of fact or law.

    B. Experience, knowledge, and education of the taxpayer.

    C. Isolated computational or transcriptional error.

    D. Reliance on an information return.

    E. Reliance on advice of a professional tax adviser or appraiser.

    F. Reliance on erroneous information.

While reliance on an information return, a tax adviser, or information that (unbeknownst to the taxpayer) is incorrect does not necessarily indicate reasonable cause and good faith, the regulations state that such reliance can constitute reasonable cause and good faith where the reliance was reasonable, and the taxpayer acted in good faith

### Penalty For Valuation Misstatement

An accuracy related penalty under IRC § 6662 applies to the portion of an underpayment of tax attributed to a valuation misstatement. Thresholds apply to determine whether a valuation misstatement arising from an IRC § 482 allocation is a substantial valuation misstatement or gross valuation misstatement, either of which may be subject to a net adjustment penalty or a transactional penalty.

**When Does the Transfer Pricing Penalty Apply?**
The penalties described in I.R.C. ' 6662(e) apply whenever there is an underpayment of tax attributable to a valuation misstatement, subject to certain thresholds.

In any year, no penalty is imposed under these rules unless the underpayment of tax attributable to all valuation misstatements exceeds a dollar limitation of $5,000 in the case of an individual, S corporation and personal holding companies (as defined by I.R.C. ' 542) or $10,000 in the case of a corporation. I.R.C. ' 6662(e)(2).
This dollar limitation must be met for each year in which the penalty will be asserted, including carryback and carryover years of any valuation misstatements. Treas. Reg. '_1.6662-5(b).

**Alteration Of a Jurat**
If there be any interlineation or erasure in the Jurat, an affidavit cannot be read or made use of.

Once individuals have sworn the affidavit, it's done. With one exception — for typos, discussed below — the only way individuals can fix a mistake in that affidavit or add additional information to it is to make a new affidavit.

**Trust Fund Recovery Penalty (TFRP)**
**Employment Taxes and the Trust Fund Recovery Penalty (TFRP)**
An employer is required by law to withhold payroll tax from employees and then send the withholding money to the IRS. The requirement to send the money to the IRS can be daily, every other day, weekly, bi-weekly, monthly, or even quarterly. At the end of each quarter the employer would file form 941 indicating to the IRS the amount of withholding for the quarter. Some employers would file 944, annual form, that is a topic for next time.

A trust fund recovery penalty is when the employer fails to send the withholding tax to the IRS.

## What Happens If an Employer Does Not Send the Money to the IRS?

It may be possible that the employer is unable to send the money to the IRS, because the employer is using the money to pay for other liabilities. The IRS will penalize anyone who made the decision not to pay the tax liability. The IRS can come after the members of the business, managers, secretary, and anyone else who has decision making ability.

The amount of penalty can be equal to the amount of money taken from the employees and not paid to the IRS.

## Penalties Imposed on The Tax Practitioner

When preparing a client's tax return, a practitioner must exercise due diligence and good faith, all while staying up to date on all IRS policies and guidelines. If they do not follow the IRS rules for preparing returns, they could be liable for penalties and fines. Such mistakes could be devastating for the client, both personally and professionally.

## Penalties For Substantial Understatement

Individuals understate their tax if the tax shown on the return is less than the correct tax. The understatement is substantial if it is more than the larger of 10 percent of the correct tax or $5,000 for individuals. For corporations, the understatement is considered substantial if the tax shown on the return exceeds the lesser of 10 percent (or if greater, $10,000) or $10,000,000.

Penalty may be asserted if individuals carelessly, recklessly or intentionally disregard IRS rules and regulations — by taking a position on the return with little or no effort to determine whether the position is correct or knowingly taking a position that is incorrect. Individuals will not have to pay a negligence penalty if there was a reasonable cause for a position they took and they acted in good faith.

However, if there is any underpayment of tax on the return due to fraud, a penalty of 75% (Civil Fraud penalty) of the underpayment due to fraud will be added to the tax. The fraud penalty on a joint return does not apply to a spouse unless some part of the underpayment is due to the fraud of that spouse. If there is strong evidence of fraud, an I.R.S. The examiner will refer the case to the Internal Revenue Service Criminal Investigation Division for possible criminal prosecution.

## Listing Of Preparer Additional Penalties and Amounts

- IRC § 6694 - Understatement of taxpayer's liability by tax return preparer

- IRC § 6694(a) - Understatement due to unreasonable position. The penalty is the greater of $1000 or 50% of the income derived by the tax return preparer with respect to the return or claim for refund.

- IRC § 6694(b) - Understatement due to willful or reckless conduct. The penalty is the greater of $5,000 or 75% of the income derived by the tax return preparer with respect to the return or claim for refund.

- IRC § 6695 – Other assessable penalties with respect to the preparation of tax returns for other persons.
- IRC § 6695(a) – Failure to furnish a copy to the taxpayer ($50 for each failure to furnish a copy of a completed return to a taxpayer.)

- IRC § 6695(b) – Failure to sign return ($50 for each failure to sign a return.)

- IRC § 6695(c) – Failure to furnish identifying number ($50 for each failure to furnish an identifying number on a return SSN, ITIN, ATIN)

- IRC § 6695(d) – Failure to retain copy or list ($50 penalty for each failure to retain a copy or list of each completed return or claim.

- IRC § 6695(e) – Failure to file correct information returns

- IRC § 6695(f) – Negotiation of check ($545 penalty for a tax return preparer who endorses or negotiates any check

- IRC § 6695(g) – Failure to be diligent in determining eligibility for certain tax benefits – Failure to be diligent in determining eligibility for certain tax benefits $545 penalty for each failure to comply with eitc, aotc, or ctc.

- IRC § 6700 – Promoting abusive tax shelters – Promoting abusive tax shelters: $1000 for each organization or sale of an abusive plan or arrangement or if lesser 100% of the income derived from the activity.

- IRC § 6701 – Penalties for aiding and abetting understatement of tax liability: $1000, $10,000 if relating to a corporation's tax return for aiding and abetting in an understatement of a tax liability.

- IRC § 6713 – Disclosure or use of information by preparers of returns - $250 for each unauthorized disclosure or use of information furnished for or in connection with the preparation of a return. The max penalty is $10,000 a year. If a disclosure or use is made in connection with a crime relating to the misappropriation of another taxpayer's identity, whether or not such crime involves any tax filing the penalty increases to $1000 for each use of disclosure, with a maximum of %50,000 per person per calendar year.

- IRC § 7206 – Fraud and false statements - Guilty of a felony and upon conviction a fine of not more than $100,000 or $500,000 in the case of a corporation, imprisonment of not more than three year or both.

- IRC § 7207 – Fraudulent returns, statements, or other documents - Guilty of a misdemeanor and upon conviction a fine of not more than $10,000 or $50,000 in the case of a corporation, imprisonment of not more than one year or both.

# Pop Quiz & Answer Sheet
# Rules & Penalties

**POP QUIZ**

Test your knowledge on *Rules & Penalties* by answering the questions below. The answer sheet may be found at the end of the Pop Quiz.

**Q1: Which authority has the power to censure, suspend, or disbar a practitioner from practicing before the IRS?**

A. The IRS Commissioner
B. The Secretary of the Treasury
C. The President of the United States
D. The Chief Justice of the Supreme Court

**Q2: What is censure?**

A. A monetary penalty
B. A temporary suspension
C. A public reprimand
D. A permanent disbarment

**Q3: What must a complaint include when filed against a practitioner or appraiser?**

A. The practitioner's educational background
B. A clear and concise description of the facts and law constituting the basis for the proceeding
C. The practitioner's client's personal information
D. The practitioner's income for the past five years

**Q4: What can happen if a practitioner fails to file an answer to a complaint within the prescribed time?**

A. The practitioner is automatically exonerated
B. The allegations are deemed admitted, and a decision by default may be rendered
C. The case is dismissed
D. The practitioner is given an indefinite extension

**Q5: How long must a practitioner retain copies of communications sent to clients, such as direct mail or e-commerce messages?**

A. 1 year
B. 2 years
C. 3 years
D. 4 years

**Q6: Which of the following is not considered a "reasonable cause" for avoiding an accuracy-related penalty?**

A. Reliance on the advice of a professional tax adviser
B. Isolated computational or transcriptional error
C. Consistent underreporting of income
D. Reliance on an information return

**Q7: Which of the following actions is NOT considered disreputable conduct under Circular 230?**

A. Conviction of any criminal offense involving dishonesty or breach of trust
B. Willfully failing to make a federal tax return in violation of the Federal tax laws
C. Accurately reporting all income and deductions on a tax return

D. Knowingly aiding and abetting another person to practice before the IRS during a period of suspension

**Q8: What is the penalty for a practitioner who fails to provide information requested by the IRS during an investigation into their conduct?**

A. Automatic suspension from practice
B. Public reprimand
C. Financial penalty only
D. Potential censure, suspension, or disbarment

**Q9: What must a practitioner do if they become aware of a client's non-compliance with the revenue laws?**

A. Immediately notify the IRS
B. Inform the client of the non-compliance and advise them of the consequences
C. Ignore the issue if it is minor
D. Fix the client's tax return without informing them

**Q10: Under Circular 230, which of the following is required for a practitioner when giving written advice on Federal tax matters?**

A. Must charge a contingent fee for the advice
B. Base the advice on reasonable factual and legal assumptions
C. Guarantee the outcome of the advice given
D. Provide the advice verbally only

**Q11: If a practitioner has a conflict of interest, under what condition can they still represent a client before the IRS?**

A.If they charge a higher fee for the service
B.If each affected client gives informed consent, confirmed in writing

C.If they do not inform the IRS of the conflict
D.If the conflict of interest is minor

# Answer Sheet
# Rules & Penalties

## Question 1:

- **Answer:** B. The Secretary of the Treasury
- **Explanation:** The Secretary of the Treasury, or their delegate, has the authority to censure, suspend, or disbar any practitioner from practice before the IRS.

## Question 2:

- **Answer:** C. A public reprimand
- **Explanation:** Censure is a public reprimand issued to a practitioner for violating regulations.

## Question 3:

- **Answer:** B. A clear and concise description of the facts and law constituting the basis for the proceeding
- **Explanation:** A complaint must provide a clear and concise description of the facts and law that constitute the basis for the proceeding against the practitioner or appraiser.

## Question 4:

- **Answer:** B. The allegations are deemed admitted, and a decision by default may be rendered
- **Explanation:** Failure to file an answer within the prescribed time constitutes an admission of the allegations, and a decision by default may be rendered against the respondent.

## Question 5:

- **Answer:** C. 3 years

- **Explanation:** Practitioners must retain copies of the actual communication and a list or description of persons to whom the communication was sent for at least 36 months from the date of the last transmission or use.

## Question 6:

- **Answer:** C. Consistent underreporting of income
- **Explanation:** Consistent underreporting of income is not considered a "reasonable cause" and can lead to penalties. Reasonable cause includes isolated errors, reliance on advice, or reliance on an information return.

## Question 7:

- **Answer:** C. Accurately reporting all income and deductions on a tax return
- **Explanation:** Accurately reporting all income and deductions on a tax return is compliant behavior, not disreputable conduct.

## Question 8:

- **Answer:** D. Potential censure, suspension, or disbarment
- **Explanation:** Failing to provide requested information during an investigation can led to censure, suspension, or disbarment as it is considered non-compliance with IRS regulations.

## Question 9:

- **Answer:** B. Inform the client of the non-compliance and advise them of the consequences
- **Explanation:** The practitioner must promptly advise the client of the non-compliance, error, or omission, and the consequences as provided under the Code and regulations.

## Question 10:

- **Answer:** B. Base the advice on reasonable factual and legal assumptions

- **Explanation:** Written advice must be based on reasonable factual and legal assumptions, considering all relevant facts and circumstances.

## Question 11:

- **Answer:** B. If each affected client gives informed consent, confirmed in writing
- **Explanation:** A practitioner may represent a client if the conflict of interest is disclosed, and each affected client gives informed consent, confirmed in writing.

# Power of Attorney

## Overview

Taxpayers may either represent themselves, or they may authorize an individual to represent them before the IRS. If taxpayers choose to have someone to represent them, the representative must be a person eligible to do so before the IRS.

## What Is a Power of Attorney?

A power of attorney is the written authorization for an individual to receive confidential tax information from the IRS and to perform certain actions on a taxpayer's behalf. If the authorization is not limited, the individual generally can perform all acts that the taxpayer can perform, except negotiating or endorsing a check. The authority granted to enrolled retirement plan agents, enrolled actuaries and unenrolled return preparers holding records of completion is limited.

## Acts performed

Attorneys, certified public accountants, and enrolled agents may perform the following acts:
1. Represent taxpayers before any office or employee of the IRS.
2. Sign an offer or a waiver of restriction on assessment or collection of a tax deficiency, or a waiver of notice of disallowance of claim for credit or refund.
3. Sign a consent to extend the statutory time period for assessment or collection of a tax.
4. Sign a closing agreement.

The representative named under a power of attorney is not permitted to sign an income tax return unless:
      A. The signature is permitted under the

Internal Revenue Code and the related regulations (see Regulations section 1.6012-1(a)(5)), and

B. Taxpayers specifically authorize this in their power of attorney. For example, the regulation permits a representative to sign a return if the taxpayers are unable to sign the return due to:

- Disease or injury
- Continuous absence from the United States (including Puerto Rico) for a period of at least 60 days prior to the date required by law for filing the return.
- Other good cause if specific permission is requested of and granted by the IRS.
- When a return is signed by a representative, it must be accompanied by a power of attorney (or copy) authorizing the representative to sign the return. For more information, see the Instructions for Form 2848.

**When Is a Power of Attorney Required?**
Taxpayers need to submit a power of attorney when they want to authorize an individual to receive their confidential tax information and represent them before the IRS, whether or not the representative performs any of the other acts cited earlier.

A power of attorney is most often required when a taxpayer wants to authorize another individual to perform at least one of the following acts on his or her behalf:

- Represent the taxpayer at a meeting with the IRS.
- Prepare and file a written response to an IRS inquiry.

**Form Required**
Taxpayers need to use IRS Form 2848 to appoint a

recognized representative to act on their behalf before the IRS. Individuals recognized to represent them before the IRS are listed under Part II, Declaration of Representative, of Form 2848. The representative must complete that part of the form.

Taxpayers may authorize a student who works in a qualified Low Income Taxpayer Clinic (LITC) or Student Tax Clinic Program (STCP) to represent them under a special appearance authorization issued by the Taxpayer Advocate Service.

The authorization of a qualifying representative will also allow that individual to receive and inspect the taxpayer's confidential tax information.

**Purpose of Form**
Taxpayers need to use Form 2848 to authorize an individual to represent them before the IRS.

The individual that the taxpayer authorizes must be eligible to practice before the IRS. Form 2848, Part II, Declaration of Representative, lists eligible designations in items (a)–(r).

Taxpayers may authorize a student who works in a qualified Low Income Taxpayer Clinic (LITC) or Student Tax Clinic Program (STCP) to represent them under a special appearance authorization issued by the Taxpayer Advocate Service. See Qualifying students in LITCs and STCPs under Part II. Declaration of Representative, later. The authorization of an eligible representative will also allow that individual to inspect and/or receive the taxpayer's confidential tax information.

**Form 8821.** Taxpayers need to use Form 8821, Tax Information Authorization, if they want to authorize an individual or organization to inspect and/or receive their confidential tax return information, but do not want to authorize an individual to represent them before the IRS.

**Form 56.** Taxpayers need to use Form 56, Notice Concerning Fiduciary Relationship, to notify the IRS of the existence of a fiduciary relationship. A fiduciary (trustee, executor, administrator, receiver, or guardian) stands in the position of a taxpayer and acts as the taxpayer, not as a representative. A fiduciary may authorize an individual to represent or perform certain acts on behalf of the person or entity by filing a power of attorney that names the eligible individual(s) as representative(s) for the person or entity.

Because the fiduciary stands in the position of the person or entity, the fiduciary must sign the power of attorney on behalf of the person or entity.

Address information provided on Form 2848 will not change the taxpayer's last known address with the IRS. To change the last known address, taxpayers need to use Form 8822, Change of Address, for their home address and Form 8822-B, Change of Address or Responsible Party — Business, to change their business address. Both forms are available at IRS.gov.

### Where To File

If a taxpayer checks the box on line 4, he or she needs to mail or fax Form 2848 to the IRS office handling the specific matter. Otherwise, the taxpayer needs to mail or fax Form 2848 directly to the IRS address according to the Where to File Chart.

## Authority Granted

Except as specified below or in other IRS guidance, this power of attorney authorizes the listed representative(s) to inspect and/or receive confidential tax information and to perform all acts (that is, sign agreements, consents, waivers, or other documents) that the taxpayers can perform with respect to matters described in the power of attorney. Representatives are not authorized to endorse or otherwise negotiate any check (including directing or accepting payment by any means, electronic or otherwise, into an account owned or controlled by the representative or any firm or other entity with whom the representative is associated) issued by the government in respect of a federal tax liability.

Additionally, unless specifically provided in the power of attorney, this authorization does not include the power to substitute or add another representative, the power to sign certain returns, the power to execute a request for disclosure of tax returns or return information to a third party, or to access IRS records via an Intermediate Service Provider. See Line 5a. Additional Acts Authorized, later, for more information regarding specific authorities.

The power to sign tax returns may only be granted in limited situations. See Line 5a. Additional Acts Authorized, later, for more information.

## Revocation of Power of Attorney/Withdrawal of Representative

**Revocation by taxpayer.** If the taxpayers want to revoke a previously executed power of attorney and do not want to name a new representative, they must write "REVOKE" across the top of the first page with a current signature and date below this annotation. Then, the taxpayers must mail or fax a copy of the power of attorney with the revocation annotation to the IRS, using the Where to File Chart, or if the power of attorney is for a specific matter, to the IRS office handling the matter.

If the taxpayers do not have a copy of the power of attorney they want to revoke, they must send the IRS a statement of revocation that indicates the authority of the power of attorney is revoked, lists the matters and years/periods, and lists the name and address of each recognized representative whose authority is revoked. Taxpayers must sign and date this statement. If they are completely revoking authority, write "remove all years/periods" instead of listing the specific matters and years/periods.

**Withdrawal by representative.** If the representative wants to withdraw from representation, he or she must write "WITHDRAW" across the top of the first page of the power of attorney with a current signature and date below the annotation. Then, he or she must provide a copy of the power of attorney with the withdrawal annotation to the IRS in the same manner described in Revocation by taxpayer above.

If the representative does not have a copy of the power of attorney he or she wants to withdraw, he or she must send the IRS a statement of withdrawal that indicates the authority of the power of attorney is withdrawn, lists the matters and years/periods, and lists the name, TIN, and address (if known) of the taxpayer. The representative must sign and date this statement.

## Substitute Form 2848
The IRS will accept a power of attorney other than

Form 2848 provided the document satisfies the requirements for a power of attorney. These alternative powers of attorney cannot, however, be recorded on the CAF unless the taxpayers attach a completed Form 2848. Taxpayers are not required to sign Form 2848 when they attach it to an alternative power of attorney that they have signed, but the representative must sign the form in Part II, Declaration of Representative.

## Representative Address Change

If the representative's address has changed, the IRS does not require a new Form 2848. The representative can send a written notification that includes the new information and the representative's signature to the location with the Form 2848.

## Durable Power of Attorney

Durable power of attorney: A power of attorney that is not subject to a time limit and that will continue in force after the incapacitation or incompetency of the principal (the taxpayer).

## Retention/Revocation of Prior Power(s) of Attorney

A newly filed power of attorney concerning the same matter will revoke a previously filed power of attorney. However, the new power of attorney will not revoke the prior power of attorney if it specifically states it does not revoke such prior power of attorney and either of the following are attached to the new power of attorney.

A copy of the unrevoked prior power of attorney, or A statement signed by the taxpayer listing the name and address of each representative authorized under the prior unrevoked power of attorney.

Note. The filing of Form 2848 will not revoke any Form 8821 that is in effect.

## Updating A Power of Attorney

Taxpayers need to submit any update or modification to an existing power of attorney in writing. The signature (or the signature of the individual(s) authorized to sign on the taxpayer's behalf) is required. This can be done by sending the updated Form 2848 or non-IRS power of attorney to the IRS office(s) where the taxpayers previously sent the original(s), including the service center where the related return was, or will be filed.

A recognized representative may substitute or delegate authority if the taxpayers specifically authorize their representative to substitute or delegate representation in the original power of attorney. To make a substitution or delegation, the representative must file the following items with the IRS office(s) where the power of attorney was filed.

- A written notice of substitution or delegation signed by the recognized representative.
- A written declaration of representation made by the new representative.
- A copy of the power of attorney that specifically authorizes the substitution or delegation

## Representative Signing In Lieu Of The Taxpayer

### Acts performed

Attorneys, certified public accountants, and enrolled agents may perform the following acts:

1. Represent taxpayers before any office or employee of the IRS.
2. Sign an offer or a waiver of restriction on assessment or collection of a tax deficiency, or a waiver of notice of disallowance of claim for credit or refund.
3. Sign a consent to extend the statutory time period for assessment or collection of a tax.

4. Sign a closing agreement.

## Representing a Decedent

Form 56 should be filed by a fiduciary to notify the IRS of the creation or termination of a fiduciary relationship under section 6903. For example, if you are acting as fiduciary for an individual, a decedent's estate, or a trust, you may file Form 56.

Do not use Form 56 if you are notifying the IRS that you are the authorized representative of the taxpayer. Instead, use Form 2848, Power of Attorney and Declaration of Representative.

A fiduciary is treated by the IRS as if he or she is actually the taxpayer. Upon appointment, the fiduciary automatically has both the right and the responsibility to undertake all actions the taxpayer is required to perform. For example, the fiduciary must file returns and pay any taxes due on behalf of the taxpayer.

An authorized representative is treated by the IRS as the agent of the taxpayer. He or she can only perform the duties authorized by the taxpayer, as indicated on Form 2848. An authorized representative is not required nor permitted to do anything other than the actions explicitly authorized by the taxpayer.

**For example:** You have a client that passed away. You help their beneficiary who is the executor of the estate file form 56 to name them as the fiduciary. This gives them the right to act on behalf of the decedent's estate. You as their Enrolled Agent will file form 2848 Power of Attorney so that you can represent the fiduciary who is representing the decedent's estate.

## Tax Information Authorization Form 8821

Taxpayers Can File Form 8821 to Authorize any individual, corporation, firm, organization, or partnership designated to inspect and/or receive their confidential information verbally or in writing for the type of tax and the years or periods listed on the form.

Taxpayers Can File Form 8821 to Delete or revoke prior tax information authorizations.

**Purpose of Form**

Form 8821 authorizes any individual, corporation, firm, organization, or partnership designated to inspect and/or receive the taxpayer's confidential information verbally or in writing for the type of tax and the years or periods listed on Form 8821. Form 8821 is also used to delete or revoke prior tax information authorizations. See the instructions for line 6, later.

Taxpayers may file their own tax information authorization without using Form 8821, but it must include all the information that is requested on Form 8821.

Form 8821 doesn't authorize the appointee to speak on the taxpayer's behalf; to execute a request to allow disclosure of return or return information to another third party; to advocate the position with respect to federal tax laws; to execute waivers, consents, closing agreements; or represent the taxpayer in any other manner before the IRS. Use Form 2848, Power of Attorney and Declaration of Representative, to authorize an individual to represent the taxpayer before the IRS. The appointee may not substitute another party as an authorized designee.

Authorizations listed on prior Forms 8821 are automatically revoked unless the taxpayer attaches copies of the prior Forms 8821 to his or her new submissions.

## When to File

If taxpayers are submitting Form 8821 to authorize disclosure of their confidential tax information for a purpose other than addressing or resolving a tax matter with the IRS (for example, for income verification required by a lender), the IRS must receive the Form 8821 within 120 days of the taxpayer's signature date on the form.

This 120-day requirement doesn't apply to a Form 8821 submitted to authorize disclosure for the purpose of assistance with a tax matter with the IRS.

## Where to File

If a taxpayer checks the box on line 4, he or she needs to mail, or fax Form 8821 to the IRS office handling the specific matter. Otherwise, the taxpayer needs to mail, or fax Form 8821 directly to the IRS address according to the Where to File Chart.

## Specific Instructions

### Line 1. Taxpayer Information
Address information provided on Form 8821 will not change the last known address with the IRS. To change the last known address, taxpayers need to use Form 8822 for their home address and Form 8822-B to change their business address.

- Individuals. Enter the name, TIN, and the street address in the space provided. Don't enter the appointee's name or address information in the Taxpayer information box. If a return is a joint return, the appointee(s) identified will only be authorized for the taxpayer. The spouse, or former spouse, must submit a separate Form

8821 to designate an appointee.

- Corporation, partnership, or association. Enter the name, EIN, and business address.
- Employee plan or exempt organization. Enter the name, address, and EIN or SSN of the plan sponsor/plan name, exempt organization or bond issuer. Enter the three-digit plan number when applicable. If a taxpayer is the plan's trustee and he or she is authorizing the IRS to disclose the tax information of the plan's trust, see the instructions relating to the trust.
- Trust. Enter the name, title, and address of the trustee, and the name and EIN of the trust.
- Estate. Enter the name and address of the estate. If the estate doesn't have a separate taxpayer identification number, enter the decedent's SSN or ITIN.

## Line 2. Appointee

- Enter the appointee's full name and mailing address. Use the identical full name on all submissions and correspondence. Enter the nine-digit CAF number for each appointee. If an appointee has a CAF number for any previously filed Form 8821 or power of attorney (Form 2848), use that number. If a CAF number has not been assigned, enter "NONE," and the IRS will issue one directly to the appointee. The IRS doesn't assign CAF numbers for employee plan status determination or exempt organization application requests.
- If a taxpayer wants to name more than one appointee, he or she needs to check the box on line 2, and to attach a list of appointees to Form 8821. The taxpayer needs to provide the address and requested numbers for each appointee named.
- Taxpayers need to check the appropriate box to indicate if the appointee's address, telephone

number, or fax number is new since the IRS issued the CAF number.

- Penalties for unauthorized disclosures. Appointees receiving tax information pursuant to a tax information authorization may be subject to penalties for unauthorized uses and disclosures of such information.

## Line 3. Tax Information

- Authority to access electronic IRS records via Intermediate Service Providers. The appointee is not authorized to use an Intermediate Service Provider to retrieve confidential tax information indirectly from the IRS unless the taxpayer checks the box on line 3. If the taxpayer doesn't authorize the use of an Intermediate Service Provider, the appointee can obtain the tax information directly from the IRS by using the IRS e-Services Transcript Delivery System.
- Intermediate Service Providers are privately owned companies that offer subscriptions to their software and/or services that the authorized appointee can use to retrieve, store, and display the tax return data (personal or business) instead of obtaining the tax information directly from the IRS through the IRS e-Services Transcript Delivery System. Intermediate Service Providers are independent of, and not affiliated in any way with, the IRS, and the IRS has no involvement in the appointee's choice to obtain the tax information directly from the IRS or use an Intermediate Service Provider to indirectly obtain the tax information from the IRS.
- Columns (a)–(c). Enter the type of tax information, the tax form number, the years or periods, and the specific matter. For example, the taxpayers may list "Income, 1040" for calendar year "2018" and "Excise, 720" for "2018" (this covers all quarters in 2018).
- For multiple years or a series of inclusive periods,

including quarterly periods, the taxpayers may enter, for example, "2017 thru 2019" or "2nd 2017-3rd 2018." For fiscal years, enter the ending year and month, using the YYYYMM format.

- Don't use a general reference such as "All years," "All periods," or "All taxes." Any tax information authorization with a general reference will be returned.
- Taxpayers may list the current year/period and any tax years or periods that have already ended as of the date they sign the tax information authorization.
- Taxpayers may also list future tax years or periods. However, the IRS will not record on the CAF system future tax years or periods listed that exceed 3 years from December 31 of the year that the IRS receives the tax information authorization.

**CAF Number**

A CAF number is a unique nine-digit identification number and is assigned the first time you file a third-party authorization with the IRS. A letter is sent to you informing you of your assigned CAF number. Use your assigned CAF number on all future authorizations.

CAF numbers are different from the third party's TIN (Taxpayer Identification Number), EIN (Employer Identification Number) or PTIN (Preparer Identification Number). CAF numbers may be assigned to an individual or a business entity.

If you are a tax professional and cannot remember your CAF number, you may call the Practitioner Priority Service, otherwise known as PPS. PPS may be reached at 866-860-4259. A PPS assistor will initiate the process to help you retrieve your CAF number once you provide your authenticating information.

CAF number: The Centralized Authorization File number issued by the IRS to each representative whose power of attorney, and each designee whose tax information authorization, has been recorded on the CAF system.

Centralized Authorization File (CAF) System: The computer file system containing information regarding the authority of individuals appointed under powers of attorney or persons designated under the tax information authorization system. This system gives IRS personnel quicker access to authorization information.

**Tax Return Copies and Transcripts**

The IRS recommends that taxpayers keep a copy of tax returns for at least three years. Doing so can help taxpayers prepare future tax returns or even assist with amending a prior year's return. If a taxpayer is unable to locate copies of previous year tax returns, they should check with their software provider or tax preparer first. Tax returns are available from the IRS for a fee.

Even though taxpayers may have a copy of their tax return, some taxpayers need a transcript. These are often necessary for a mortgage or college financial aid application.

Here is some information about copies of tax returns and transcripts that can help taxpayers know when and how to get them:

To get a transcript, taxpayers can:
- Order online. They can use the Get Transcript tool on IRS.gov. Users must authenticate their identity with the Secure Access process.
- Order by mail. Taxpayers can use Get Transcript by Mail or call
- 800-908-9946 to order tax return transcripts and tax account transcripts.
- Complete and send either 4506-T or 4506T-EZ to the

IRS. They should use Form 4506-T to request other tax records, such as a tax account transcript, record of account, wage and income, and a verification of non-filing.

Transcripts are free and available for the current tax year and the past three years.

A transcript usually displays most line items from the tax return. This includes marital status, the type of return filed, adjusted gross income and taxable income. It also includes items from any related forms and schedules filed. It doesn't reflect any changes the taxpayer or the IRS may have made to the original return.

Taxpayers needing a transcript should remember to plan ahead. Delivery times for online and phone orders typically take five to 10 days from the time the IRS receives the request. Taxpayers should allow 30 days to receive a transcript ordered by mail, and 75 days for copies of the tax return.

**Copies of tax returns**

Taxpayers who need an actual copy of a tax return can get one for the current tax year and as far back as six years. The fee per copy is $50. A taxpayer will complete and mail Form 4506 to request a copy of a tax return. They should mail the request to the appropriate IRS office listed on the form.

Taxpayers who live in a federally declared disaster area can get a free copy of their tax return. More disaster relief information is available on IRS.gov.

For those that need tax transcripts, however, the IRS can help. Transcripts are free.

**Tax Transcripts**

- A transcript summarizes return information and includes Adjusted Gross Income (AGI). They are available for the most current tax year after the IRS has processed the return. People can also get them for the past three years.
- When applying for home mortgages or college financial aid, transcripts are often necessary. Mortgage companies, however, normally arrange to get one for a homeowner or potential homeowner. For people applying for college financial aid, see IRS Offers Help to Students, Families to Get Tax Information for Student Financial Aid Applications on IRS.gov for the latest options.

**To get a transcript, people can:**

- Order online. Use the 'Get Transcript' tool available on IRS.gov. There is a link to it under the red TOOLS bar on the front page. Those who use it must authenticate their identity using the Secure Access process.
- Order by phone. The number to call is 800-908-9946.
- Order by mail. Complete and send either Form 4506-T or Form 4506T-EZ to the IRS to get one by mail. Use Form 4506-T to request other tax records: tax account transcript, record of account, wage and income and verification of non-filing. These forms are available on the Forms & Pubs page on IRS.gov

Those who need an actual copy of a tax return can get one for the current tax year and as far back as six years. The fee per copy is $50. Complete and mail Form 4506 to request a copy of a tax return. Mail the request to the appropriate IRS office listed on the form. People who live in a federally declared disaster area can get a free copy.

**Plan ahead.** Delivery times for online and phone orders typically take five to 10 days from the time the IRS receives the request. Individuals should allow 30 days to receive a transcript ordered by mail and 75 days for copies of the tax returns.

### Transcript Types

The IRS offers the following transcript types at no charge:

**Tax Return Transcript** - shows most line items including the adjusted gross income (AGI) from the original tax return (Form 1040, 1040A or 1040EZ) as filed, along with any forms and schedules. It doesn't show changes made after the original return is filed. This transcript is only available for the current tax year and returns processed during the prior three years. A tax return transcript usually meets the needs of lending institutions offering mortgages and student loans. Note: the secondary spouse on a joint return must use Get Transcript Online or Form 4506-T to request this transcript type. When using Get Transcript by Mail or phone, the primary taxpayer on the return must make the request.

**Tax Account Transcript** - shows basic data such as return type, marital status, adjusted gross income, taxable income and all payment types. It also shows changes made after the original return is filed. This transcript is available for the current tax year and up to 10 prior years using Get Transcript Online or Form 4506-T. When using Get Transcript by Mail or phone, individuals are limited to the current tax year and returns processed during the prior three years. Note: If individuals made estimated tax payments and/or applied an overpayment from a prior year return, they can request this transcript type a few weeks after the beginning of the calendar year to confirm the payments prior to filing the tax return.

**Record of Account Transcript** - combines the tax return and tax account transcripts above into one complete transcript. This transcript is available for the current tax year and returns processed during the prior three years using Get Transcript Online or Form 4506-T.

**Wage and Income Transcript** - shows data from information returns we receive such as Forms W-2, 1099, 1098 and Form 5498, IRA Contribution Information. Current tax year information may not be complete until July. This transcript is available for up to 10 prior years using Get Transcript Online or Form 4506-T. Verification of Non-filing Letter - provides proof that the IRS has no record of a filed Form 1040, 1040A or 1040EZ for the year requested. It doesn't indicate whether individuals were required to file a return for that year. This letter is available after June 15 for the current tax year or anytime for the prior three tax years using Get Transcript Online or Form 4506-T. Individuals must use Form 4506-T if they need a letter for tax years older than the prior three years.

**Note:** A transcript can show return and/or account data. It also can show changes or transactions made after individuals filed the original return. Transaction codes consist of three digits. They are used to identify a transaction being processed and to maintain a history of actions posted to a taxpayer's account.

**Note:** A transcript isn't a photocopy of the return. If taxpayers need a copy of the original return, complete and mail Form 4506, Request for Copy of Tax Return, along with the applicable fee.

**Privacy Of Taxpayer Information**

When dealing with the IRS, taxpayers have the right to confidentiality. As with all ten rights outlined in the Taxpayer Bill of Rights, the IRS takes this right seriously.

Taxpayers can expect that any information they provide to the IRS will not be disclosed to outside parties, unless authorized by the taxpayer or by law. Taxpayers have the right to expect appropriate action will be taken against employees, return preparers and others who wrongfully use or disclose taxpayer return information.

Here are some more things that taxpayers can expect when it comes to the right to confidentiality:

- In general, the IRS may not disclose a taxpayer's tax information to third parties, unless those taxpayers give the agency permission. Examples of when a taxpayer requests that the IRS discloses this information could be regarding a mortgage or student loan application.
- In general, the IRS cannot contact third parties, such as a taxpayer's employer, neighbor, or bank, to get information about a taxpayer unless it provides the taxpayer with reasonable notice before making the contact.
- When dealing with a federally authorized tax practitioner, taxpayers can expect the same confidentiality protection that they would have with an attorney.

Here are a couple of examples of communications with a practitioner that are considered confidential:

- The preparer advises the taxpayer about their dealings with the IRS.
- Issues related to noncriminal tax matters before the IRS.
- A tax preparer cannot disclose or use someone's tax information for any reason other than for tax return preparation. A preparer who does this may be subject to criminal fines and prison.

**Third-Party Designee**

Taxpayers can allow the IRS to discuss their tax return information with a third party by completing the Third-Party Designee section of the tax return, often referred to as "Checkbox Authority." This will allow the IRS to discuss the processing of the current tax return, including the status of tax refunds, with the designated person. This authorization is limited to matters concerning the processing of the tax return containing the completed Third Party Designee section. The third-party designee authority only lasts one year from the due date of the return, except for Form 709 which expires three years from the date of filing. For more information regarding third party designee, see the instructions to the individual income or business tax return individuals are filing.

This "Checkbox Authority" does not replace Form 2848, Power of Attorney and Declaration of Representative (PDF) or Form 8821, Tax Information Authorization (PDF). For more information on powers of attorney and Form 2848, refer to Topic No. 311 and to Publication 947, Practice Before the IRS and Power of Attorney.

**Oral Authorization**

In certain circumstances, the IRS can accept oral authorization from taxpayers to discuss their confidential tax return information with third parties.

For example, if a taxpayer brings another person with him or her, such as the return preparer, to an interview with the IRS or involve another person in a telephone conversation with the IRS, the IRS can disclose the confidential tax return information to that third party after confirming the identity and the identity of the third party, as well as confirming with the taxpayer the issues or matters to be discussed and what confidential tax return information the IRS may disclose in order to enable the third party to assist the taxpayer .

An oral authorization is limited to the conversation in which the taxpayer provides the authorization. Unless it is stated otherwise, the oral authorization is automatically revoked once the conversation has ended. The IRS cannot subsequently discuss the confidential tax return information with any third party until it receives a new authorization.

Form 8821 can be used for the authorization to disclose confidential tax return information in situations where continued communication with the designated third party is necessary.

**Disclosure Consent Not Required**

**Purpose of Form**

Form 8275 is used by taxpayers and tax return preparers to disclose items or positions, except those taken contrary to a regulation, that are not otherwise adequately disclosed on a tax return to avoid certain penalties. The form is filed to avoid the portions of the accuracy-related penalty due to disregard of rules or to a substantial understatement of income tax for non-tax shelter items if the return position has a reasonable basis. It can also be used for disclosures relating to the economic substance penalty and the preparer penalties for tax understatements due to unreasonable positions or disregard of rules.

The portion of the accuracy-related penalties attributable to the following types of misconduct cannot be avoided by disclosure on Form 8275.

- Negligence.
- Disregard of regulations.
- Any substantial understatement of income tax on a tax shelter item.
- Any substantial valuation misstatement under chapter 1.
- Any substantial overstatement of pension liabilities.
- Any substantial estate or gift tax valuation understatements.
- Any claim of tax benefits from a transaction lacking economic substance (within the meaning of section 7701(o)) or failing to meet the requirement of any similar rule of law.

**Exception to filing Form 8275.**
Guidance is published annually in a revenue procedure in the Internal Revenue Bulletin that identifies circumstances when an item reported on a return is considered adequate disclosure for purposes of the substantial understatement aspect of the accuracy-related penalty and for avoiding the preparer's penalty relating to understatements due to unreasonable positions.

Individuals do not have to file Form 8275 for items that meet the requirements listed in this revenue procedure. This revenue procedure can be found on the internet at IRS.gov.


**Tax Practitioner Confidentiality Privilege**

Under the modified policy of restraint, if a document is otherwise privileged under the attorney-client privilege, the Code section 7525 tax advice privilege, or the work product doctrine and the document was provided to an independent auditor as part of an audit of the taxpayer's financial statements, the IRS will not assert during an examination that privilege has been waived by such disclosure. The modified policy of restraint applies to all examinations, notwithstanding whether a Schedule UTP has been, will be, or is required to be, filed.

Accordingly, LB&I examiners cannot request, in any open examination, documents that are privileged under the attorney-client privilege, the tax advice privilege, or the work product doctrine, notwithstanding whether these documents have been provided to an independent auditor as part of a financial statement audit unless the privilege has been otherwise waived. Any outstanding requests for such documents should be withdrawn.

As a reminder, the modified policy of restraint also changed the previously existing policy of restraint in the following important way:

Taxpayers may redact the following information from any copies of tax reconciliation workpapers they are asked to produce during an examination:

Working drafts, revisions, or comments concerning the concise description of tax positions reported on Schedule UTP.

The amount of any reserve related to a tax position reported on Schedule UTP. Computations determining the ranking of tax positions to be reported on Schedule UTP or the designation of a tax position as a Major Tax Position.

**Certified Acceptance Agents**

You can apply for an Individual Taxpayer Identification Number (ITIN) in-person using the services of an IRS-authorized Certified Acceptance Agent (CAA). This will prevent you from having to mail your proof of identity and foreign status documents. After processing, the IRS will mail your ITIN to you allowing you to file the Form 1040 tax returns. The IRS works collaboratively with community-based organizations and nonprofits to offer the services of Certifying Acceptance Agents.

You may contact one of the following IRS Volunteer Income Tax Assistance partners listed below to schedule an appointment for CAA services. Also, the VITA program offers free tax help to people who generally make $56,000 or less, persons with disabilities and limited English speaking taxpayers who need assistance in preparing their own tax returns. IRS-certified volunteers provide free basic income tax return preparation with electronic filing to qualified individuals.

**The CAA Program**

The Internal Revenue Service (IRS) has implemented a change to the list of document types that Certifying Acceptance Agents (CAAs) are authorized to authenticate and submit with Individual Taxpayer Identification Number (ITIN) client's applications. A recent audit by the Treasury Inspector General for Tax Administration found there was no forensic training on foreign military identification cards available to CAAs.

Based on these findings, the IRS has eliminated the

foreign military identification card from the list of 13 types of documents that a CAA may authenticate for an ITIN application. Foreign military identification cards represent a nominal percentage of submissions from all applicants. After the proposed change is implemented, applicants will continue to be able to use these documents to obtain ITINs if they present them directly to the IRS either by mail or in person at a Taxpayer Assistance Center.

**Certification Process Changes**

CAAs can now authenticate the passport and birth certificate for dependents. CAAs will continue to certify identification documents for the primary and secondary applicants. Form W-7 (COA), Certificate of Accuracy for IRS Individual Identification Taxpayer Number, must be attached to each Form W-7 application submitted as verification they have reviewed the original documentation or certified copies from the agency that issued them. CAAs will have to attach and send copies of all documentation reviewed with the Form W-7 COA to the IRS.

As a reminder, AAs and CAAs must conduct an in-person interview with each applicant (primary, secondary and dependent) in order to complete the application. Video conferencing (i.e., SKYPE) can be used if the CAA has the original identification documents or certified copies from the agency that issued them in their possession during the interview.

ITIN Acceptance Agent Applications Accepted Year Round

Form 13551, Application to Participate in the IRS Acceptance Agent Program, is now accepted year-round.

# Certifying Acceptance Agent Recruitment

The Service is actively recruiting Certifying Acceptance Agents. The goal is to increase the availability of individual ITIN services nationwide, particularly in communities with high ITIN usage. A Certifying Acceptance Agent is a person or an entity (business or organization) who, pursuant to a written agreement with the IRS, is authorized to assist individuals and other foreign persons who do not qualify for a Social Security Number but who still need a Taxpayer Identification Number (TIN) to file a Form 1040 and other tax schedules. The Certifying Acceptance Agent facilitates the application process by reviewing the necessary documents, authenticating the identity when able and forwarding the completed forms to the IRS.

There are four steps that need to be taken by all new and renewing applicants.

- Complete Form 13551 (PDF), Application to Participate in the IRS Acceptance Agent Program, and attach the fingerprint card (if applicable).
- Complete the Mandatory Acceptance Agent training, print, sign and submit the certification form.
- Attach the certification form for each authorized representative (person listed in block 5 of the application) to Form 13551.
- Complete forensic training and submit the certificate of completion to the IRS. (CAA applicants only)

Additionally: Applications received without the required certification form(s) will not be processed.

All Acceptance Agents are required to submit at least five W-7 applications a year to remain in the program.

Background checks and tax compliance checks will be conducted by the IRS after the application is received.

Send Form 13551, along with the completed fingerprint card or evidence of professional status if required, forensic documentation, and mandatory training certification to:

## Additional Acceptance

## Agent Requirements

To ensure that Acceptance Agents have the tools they need to perform their jobs, all new and renewing applicants are required to complete mandatory training. The training session is available online. New and Renewing CAA applicants are also required to complete formal Forensic Document Training to obtain the necessary skills to determine the authenticity of identification documents. The original certificate of completion must be attached to the application Form 13551, Application to Participate in the IRS Acceptance Agent Program. For more information see: Forensic Training.

## Compliance Reviews

The IRS will conduct compliance reviews including both physical and correspondence reviews. Certifying Acceptance Agents are required to cooperate with IRS compliance checks as well as requests for information from the Treasury Inspector General for Tax Administration or the Government Accountability Office. Failure to do so can result in termination from the program.

## Quality Standards

All Acceptance Agents will be required to adhere to new quality standards established and monitored by the IRS. The focus of the new standards will be on the quality of each agent's W-7 submissions as well as their adherence to the terms and conditions of their Acceptance Agent Agreement.

These changes and requirements are designed to strengthen the ITIN program and improve service to both Acceptance Agents and their clients. Questions about the IRS Acceptance Agent Program can be directed to the ITIN Policy Section by email at ITINProgramOffice@irs.gov.

# Pop Quiz &Answer Sheet
# Power of Attorney

## POP QUIZ

Test your knowledge on *Power of Attorney* by answering the questions below. The answer sheet may be found at the end of the Pop Quiz.

**Q1: Which form should a taxpayer use to authorize an individual to represent them before the IRS and to receive their confidential tax information?**

A. Form 8821
B. Form 2848
C. Form 4506-T
D. Form 56

**Q2: What must a taxpayer do to revoke a previously executed power of attorney without naming a new representative?**

A. Submit Form 8821
B. Write "REVOKE" across the top of the first page of the power of attorney and mail or fax it to the IRS
C. Submit a new Form 2848
D. File Form 56

**Q3: What is the purpose of Form 8821?**

A. To authorize an individual to represent a taxpayer before the IRS
B. To authorize an individual or organization to inspect and/or receive a taxpayer's confidential tax return information
C. To notify the IRS of the creation or termination of a fiduciary relationship
D. To request a copy of a tax return

**Q4: Which of the following actions can an attorney, CPA, or enrolled agent NOT perform unless specifically authorized in the power of attorney?**

A. Sign a consent to extend the statutory time period for assessment or collection of a tax
B. Represent the taxpayer at a meeting with the IRS
C. Sign an income tax return
D. Sign a closing agreement

**Q5: What is the maximum number of years in the future for which the IRS will record tax years or periods listed on a tax information authorization?**

A. 1 year
B. 2 years
C. 3 years
D. 5 years

**Q6: When is a power of attorney required to be submitted to the IRS?**

A. When a taxpayer wants to authorize another individual to prepare their tax return
B. When a taxpayer wants to authorize another individual to receive their refund check
C. When a taxpayer wants to authorize another individual to represent them before the IRS and receive their confidential tax information
D. When a taxpayer wants to authorize another individual to receive a transcript of their tax return

**Q7: What information is required to be included on Form 8821?**

A. The taxpayer's name, TIN, and address
B. The appointee's name, address, and CAF number
C. The type of tax information, tax form number, and years or periods
D. All of the above

**Q8: Which form is used to notify the IRS of the creation or termination of a fiduciary relationship?**

A. Form 2848
B. Form 8821
C. Form 56
D. Form 4506-T

**Q9: What is the "Checkbox Authority" on a tax return?**

A. It authorizes the IRS to disclose tax return information to a third party for one year from the due date of the return.
B. It replaces the need for Form 2848.
C. It authorizes the appointee to sign the tax return on behalf of the taxpayer.
D. It allows the appointee to represent the taxpayer in all tax matters before the IRS.

**Q10: How long should a taxpayer keep a copy of their tax returns according to the IRS recommendation?**

A. At least 1 year
B. At least 2 years
C. At least 3 years
D. At least 6 years

# Answer Sheet
# Rules & Penalties

## Question 1:

- **Answer:** B. Form 2848

- **Explanation:** Form 2848, Power of Attorney and Declaration of Representative is used to authorize an individual to represent a taxpayer before the IRS and to receive their confidential tax information.

## Question 2:

- **Answer:** B. Write "REVOKE" across the top of the first page of the power of attorney and mail or fax it to the IRS

- **Explanation:** To revoke a previously executed power of attorney, the taxpayer must write "REVOKE" across the top of the first page of the power of attorney with a current signature and date, and mail or fax it to the IRS.

## Question 3:

- **Answer:** B. To authorize an individual or organization to inspect and/or receive a taxpayer's confidential tax return information

- **Explanation:** Form 8821 is used to authorize an individual or organization to inspect and/or receive a taxpayer's confidential tax return information.

## Question 4:

- **Answer:** C. Sign an income tax return

- **Explanation:** An attorney, CPA, or enrolled agent cannot sign an income tax return unless specifically authorized in the power of attorney and permitted under the Internal Revenue Code and related regulations.

## Question 5:

- **Answer:** C. 3 years

- **Explanation:** The IRS will not record future tax years or periods listed on a tax information authorization if they exceed 3 years from December 31 of the year the IRS receives the authorization.

## Question 6:

- **Answer:** C. When a taxpayer wants to authorize another individual to represent them before the IRS and receive their confidential tax information

- **Explanation:** A power of attorney is required when a taxpayer wants to authorize another individual to represent them before the IRS and receive their confidential tax information.

## Question 7:

- **Answer:** D. All of the above

- **Explanation:** Form 8821 requires the taxpayer's name, TIN, and address, the appointee's name, address, and CAF number, and the type of tax information, tax form number, and years or periods.

## Question 8:

- **Answer:** C. Form 56

- **Explanation:** Form 56, Notice Concerning Fiduciary Relationship, is used to notify the IRS of the creation or termination of a fiduciary relationship.

## Question 9:

- **Answer:** A. It authorizes the IRS to disclose tax return information to a third party for one year from the due date of the return.

- **Explanation:** The "Checkbox Authority" allows the IRS to discuss the processing of the current tax return, including the status of tax refunds, with the designated person for one year from the due date of the return.

## Question 10:

- **Answer:** C. At least 3 years

- **Explanation:** The IRS recommends that taxpayers keep a copy of their tax returns for at least three years.

# Supporting Documentation

## Overview

Good records can help individuals to monitor the progress of their business, prepare their financial statements, identify sources of income, keep track of deductible expenses, keep track of the basis in property, prepare the tax returns, and support items reported on the tax returns.
Individuals may choose any recordkeeping system suited to their business that clearly shows the income and expenses. Except in a few cases, the law does not require any special kind of records. However, the type of business affects the type of records individuals need to keep for federal tax purposes.

## Supporting Documents

Purchases, sales, payroll, and other transactions in the business will generate supporting documents. Supporting documents include sales slips, paid bills, invoices, receipts, deposit slips, and canceled checks. These documents contain the information business owners need to record in their books. It is important to keep these documents because they support the entries in the books and on the tax return.
Business owners should keep them in an orderly fashion and in a safe place. For instance, organizing them by year and type of income or expense.

**The following are some of the types of records individuals should keep:**

1. Gross Receipts - are the income received from a business.
   - Cash register tapes
   - Deposit information (cash and credit sales)
   - Receipt books
   - Invoices
   - Forms 1099-MISC

2. Purchases - are the items bought and resold to customers
   - Canceled checks or other documents reflecting proof of payment/electronic funds transferred
   - Cash register tape receipts
   - Credit card receipts and statements
   - Invoices

3. The following are some of the types of records individuals should keep:
   - Expenses - are the costs incurred (other than purchases) to carry on a business
   - Canceled checks or other documents reflecting proof of payment/electronic funds transferred
   - Cash register tape receipts
   - Account statements
   - Credit card receipts and statements
   - Invoices

4. Travel, Transportation, Entertainment, and Gift Expenses - If an individual deducts travel, entertainment, gift or transportation expenses, he or she must be able to prove (substantiate) certain elements of expenses

5. Assets - are the property, such as machinery and furniture, that individuals own and use in a business

- When and how the assets are acquired
- Purchase price
- Cost of any improvements
- Section 179 deduction taken
- Deductions taken for depreciation
- Deductions taken for casualty losses, such as losses resulting from fires or storms
- How the asset is used
- When and how the asset is disposed
- Selling price
- Expenses of sale

The following documents may show this information.

- Purchase and sales invoices
- Real estate closing statements
- Canceled checks or other documents that identify payee, amount, and proof of payment/electronic funds transferred

6. Employment taxes

There are specific employment tax records business owners must keep.

## The Statute of Limitations for Records Retention

The length of time individuals should keep a document depends on the action, expense, or event which the document records. Generally, individuals must keep the records that support an item of income, deduction or credit shown on the tax return until the period of limitations for that tax return runs out.

The period of limitations is the period in which individuals can amend the tax return to claim a credit or refund, or the IRS can assess additional tax.

**Period of Limitations that apply to income tax returns**

The information below reflects the periods of limitations that apply to income tax returns. Unless otherwise stated, the years refer to the period after the return was filed. Returns filed before the due date are treated as filed on the due date.

1. Keep records for 3 years if situations (4), (5), and (6) below do not apply.
2. Keep records for 3 years from the date an individual filed his or her original return or 2 years from the date he or she paid the tax, whichever is later, if an individual files a claim for credit or refund after filing the return.
3. Keep records for 7 years if an individual files a claim for a loss from worthless securities or bad debt deduction.
4. Keep records for 6 years if an individual does not report income that he or she should report, and it is more than 25% of the gross income shown on the return.
5. Keep records indefinitely if an individual does not file a return.
6. Keep records indefinitely if an individual files a fraudulent return.
7. Keep employment tax records for at least 4 years after the date that the tax becomes due or is paid, whichever is later.

**Ask these questions before throwing away documents**

1. Are the records connected to property?

Generally, keep records relating to property until the period of limitations expires for the year in which an individual disposes of the property. Individuals must keep these records to figure any depreciation, amortization, or depletion deduction and to figure the gain or loss when they sell or otherwise dispose of the property.

2. What should be done with the records for non-tax purposes?

When the records are no longer needed for tax purposes, individuals need to keep them until they check to see if they have to keep them longer for other purposes. For example, the insurance company or creditors may require the individuals to keep them longer than the IRS does.

**Other Retention Periods**

As to the tax records, the statute of limitations period for income tax returns is generally three years. It is six years if there is a substantial understatement of gross income. A good rule to thumb is to add a year to the statute of limitations period. Using this approach, taxpayers should keep most of their income tax records for a minimum of four years, but it may be more prudent to retain them for seven years.

Regardless of the tax assessment periods, taxpayers should retain certain records for longer periods, and in some cases, indefinitely. Tax return, results of an audit by a tax authority, general ledgers, and financial statements should normally be kept indefinitely

It is also important to note that the IRS permits

taxpayers to store certain tax documents electronically. Although these IRS rules are aimed primarily as businesses and sole proprietors, they presumably apply to individuals as well. These rules permit taxpayers to convert paper documents to electronic images and maintain only the electronic files. The paper document can then be destroyed.

Certain requirements must be met to take advantage of an electronic storage system.

| Types of record | Time of period to retain |
|---|---|
| Accounting records | |
| Audit report/Annual financial statement | Permanently |
| Bank statements and deposit slips | 7 years |
| Canceled checks:<br>Fixed assets<br>Taxes (payroll related)<br>Taxes (income)<br>General<br>Payroll | Permanently<br>7 years<br>Permanently<br>7 years<br>7 years |
| Cash disbursements | Permanently |
| Cash receipts journal | Permanently |
| Chart of accounts | Permanently |
| Deeds, mortgages, bills of sales | Permanently |
| Electronic payment records | 7 years |
| Employee expenses reports | 7 years |
| Freight bills and bills of lading | 7 years |
| General journal | Permanently |
| General ledger | Permanently |
| Fixed asset record (invoices, canceled checks, depreciation schedules | Permanently |
| Types of record | Time of period to retain |
| Accounting records | |
| Inventory listings and lags | 7 years |
| Invoices: sales to customers/credit memos | 7 years |
| Patent/trademark and related papers | Permanently |
| Payroll journal | 7 years |
| Production and sales report | 7 years |
| Purchases | 7 years |
| Purchases journal | Permanently |

| Types of record | Time of period to retain |
|---|---|
| Employee benefit plan records | |
| Actuarial reports | Permanently |
| Allocation and compliance testing | 7 years |
| Brokerage/Trustee statements supporting investments | 7 years |
| Financial statements | Permanently |
| General ledgers and journals | Permanently |
| Information returns (Form 5500) | Permanently |
| Internal Revenue Service/Department of Labor Correspondence | Permanently |
| Participants communications related to distribution, termination and beneficiaries | 7 years |
| Plan and trust agreements | Permanently |

| | |
|---|---|
| Purchase orders | 7 years |
| Sales or work orders | 7 years |
| Subsidiary ledgers (accounts receivable, accounts payable, equipment) | 7 years |
| Timecards and daily time reports | 7 years |
| Training journal | Permanently |
| Trial Balance - year end | Permanently |

| Types of record | Time of period to retain |
| --- | --- |
| **Personnel records** | |
| Child labor certificates and notices | 3 years |
| Employment application (from date of termination) | 2 years |
| Employment eligibility verification (I-9 Form) | 3 years |
| Help wanted ads and job opening notices | 2 years |
| Personnel files (from date of termination) | 4 years |
| Records of job injuries causing loss of work | 5 years |
| Safety - chemical and toxic exposure records | 30 years |
| Union agreements and individual employee contacts (from date of termination) | 3 years |
| **Types of record** | **Time of period to retain** |
| **Insurance records** | |
| Accident reports and settled claims | 6 years after settlement |
| Fire inspection and safety reports | 7 years |
| Insurance policies (still in effect) | Permanently |
| Insurance policies (expired) | 7 years |
| Articles of Incorporation and Bylaws | Permanently |
| Buy-sell agreements | Permanently |
| Contracts and leases (still in effect) | Permanently |
| Contracts and leases (expired) | 7 years |
| Employment agreements | 7 years |
| Legal correspondence | Permanently |
| Minutes | Permanently |
| Partnership agreements | Permanently |

| Types of record | Time of period to retain |
| --- | --- |
| **Tax records** | |
| IRS adjustments | Permanently |
| Payroll tax returns | 7 years |
| Property basis records | Permanently |
| Sales and use tax returns | Permanently |
| Tax return and canceled checks for tax payments | Permanently |

# Pop Quiz & Answer Sheet
# Supporting Documentation

## POP QUIZ

Test your knowledge on *Supporting Documentation* by answering the questions below. The answer sheet may be found at the end of the Pop Quiz.

### Question 1:

Why is it important for individuals to keep good records for their business?

A. To monitor the progress of their business
B. To prepare their financial statements
C. To support items reported on the tax returns
D. All of the above

### Question 2:

Which of the following is NOT considered a supporting document for business transactions?

A. Sales slips
B. Invoices
C. Credit card statements
D. Personal notes

**Question 3:**

What type of record should be kept for gross receipts in a business?

A. Canceled checks
B. Invoices
C. Cash register tapes
D. Credit card receipts

**Question 4:**

For how many years should individuals generally keep records if they do not report more than 25% of their gross income?

A. 3 years
B. 4 years
C. 6 years
D. Indefinitely

**Question 5:**

Which document is NOT typically kept substantiating travel, entertainment, gift, or transportation expenses?

A. Invoices
B. Receipts
C. Credit card statements
D. Bank deposit slips

## Question 6:

When must a taxpayer keep records indefinitely?

A. If they file a fraudulent return
B. If they file a claim for a refund
C. If they dispose of an asset
D. If they purchase a new asset


## Question 7:

What should individuals do with their records when they are no longer needed for tax purposes?

A. Shred them immediately
B. Keep them for at least another year
C. Check if they need to keep them longer for non-tax purposes
D. Burn them


## Question 8:

What is the minimum period that employment tax records should be kept?

A. 2 years
B. 3 years
C. 4 years
D. 5 years

**Question 9:**

Which of the following documents should be retained indefinitely?

A. Tax returns
B. General ledgers
C. Results of an audit by a tax authority
D. All of the above


**Question 10:**

What is an advantage of using an electronic storage system for tax documents?

A. It allows for easy destruction of original documents
B. It eliminates the need to keep any records
C. It provides a backup in case of loss or damage of paper documents
D. It removes the need to follow IRS rules

# Answer Sheet
# Supporting Documentation

## Question 1:

- **Answer:** D. All of the above

- **Explanation:** Good records help individuals monitor their business progress, prepare financial statements, and support items reported on tax returns.

## Question 2:

- **Answer:** D. Personal notes

- **Explanation:** Personal notes are not considered supporting documents for business transactions, unlike sales slips, invoices, and credit card statements.

## Question 3:

- **Answer:** C. Cash register tapes

- **Explanation:** Gross receipts records include cash register tapes, which show the income received from the business.

## Question 4:

- **Answer:** C. 6 years

- **Explanation:** Individuals should keep records for 6 years if they do not report income that they should report, and it is more than 25% of the gross income shown on the return.

## Question 5:

- **Answer:** D. Bank deposit slips

- **Explanation:** Bank deposit slips are not typically used to substantiate travel, entertainment, gift, or transportation expenses.

## Question 6:

- **Answer:** A. If they file a fraudulent return

- **Explanation:** Taxpayers must keep records indefinitely if they file a fraudulent return.

## Question 7:

- **Answer:** C. Check if they need to keep them longer for non-tax purposes

- **Explanation:** Individuals should keep their records until they check if they need to retain them longer for non-tax purposes, such as for insurance or creditor requirements.

## Question 8:

- **Answer:** C. 4 years

- **Explanation:** Employment tax records should be kept for at least 4 years after the tax becomes due or is paid, whichever is later.

**Question 9:**

- **Answer:** D. All of the above

- **Explanation:** Tax returns, general ledgers, and results of an audit by a tax authority should be retained indefinitely.


**Question 10:**

- **Answer:** C. It provides a backup in case of loss or damage of paper documents

- **Explanation:** An electronic storage system provides a backup for tax documents, ensuring that information is not lost or damaged.

# The Taxpayer's Financial Situation

### Installment Agreements

Individuals can use Form 9465 to request a monthly installment agreement (payment plan) if they can't pay the full amount, they owe shown on their tax return (or on a notice the IRS sent.) Most installment agreements meet the streamlined installment agreement criteria. The maximum term for a streamlined agreement is 72 months. In certain circumstances, individuals can have longer to pay, or they can establish an agreement for an amount that is less than the amount of tax they owe.

However, before requesting a payment plan, individuals should consider other alternatives, such as getting a bank loan or using available credit, which may be less costly.

### Use Form 9465 if the taxpayer is an individual:

1. Who owes income tax on Form 1040 or 1040-SR,
2. Who is or may be responsible for a Trust Fund Recovery Penalty,
3. Who owes employment taxes (for example, as reported on Forms 941, 943, or 940) related to a sole proprietor business that is no longer in operation, or
4. Who owes an individual shared responsibility payment under the Affordable Care Act (this payment won't be assessed for months beginning after December 31, 2018). See section 5000A.

### Form 9465 don't need to be used if:

The taxpayers can pay the full amount they owe within 120 days (If they plan to pay the taxes, interest and penalties due in full within 120 days, they can save the cost of the set-up fee.

The taxpayers want to request a payment plan online, including an installment agreement or,

The taxpayers' business is still operating and owes employment or unemployment taxes. Instead, call the telephone number on the most recent notice to request an installment agreement.

## Guaranteed installment agreement.

Individuals are eligible for a guaranteed installment agreement if the tax they owe isn't more than $10,000 and:

During the past 5 tax years, individuals (and their spouse if filing a joint return) have timely filed all income tax returns and paid any income tax due and haven't entered into an installment agreement for the payment of income tax.

Individuals agree to pay the full amount they owe within 3 years and to comply with the tax laws while the agreement is in effect; and

Individuals are financially unable to pay the liability in full when due.

## Installment agreement user fees.

The IRS charges a user fee to set up an installment agreement. The amount of the user fee can vary depending on whether the taxpayers use the online payment application and how they propose to make their monthly payments.

## IRS Collection Process

The IRS has wide powers when it comes to collecting unpaid taxes. If a taxpayer does not pay in full when filing his tax return, he will receive a bill from an IRS service center. The first notice explains the balance due and demands payment in full. It will include the amount of the unpaid tax balance plus any penalties and interest calculated from the date the tax was due.

The first notice taxpayers receive will be a letter that explains the balance due and demands payment in full. It will include the amount of the tax, plus any penalties and interest accrued on the unpaid balance from the date the tax was due.

If the IRS determines that the taxpayer can't pay any of the tax debt due to a financial hardship, the IRS may temporarily delay collection by reporting the account is currently not collectible until the financial condition of the taxpayer improves. Being currently not collectible doesn't mean the debt goes away. It means the IRS has determined that the taxpayer can't afford to pay the debt at this time. Prior to approving the request to delay collection, the IRS may ask the taxpayers to complete a Collection Information Statement (Form 433-F, Form 433-A, or Form 433-B) and provide proof of the financial status (this may include information about the assets and the monthly income and expenses). If the IRS does delay collecting from the taxpayer, the debt continues to accrue penalties and interest until the debt is paid in full. The IRS may temporarily suspend certain collection actions, such as issuing a levy (explained below), until the financial condition improves. However, we may still file a Notice of Federal Tax Lien while the account is suspended.

## Bankruptcy

### Types of Bankruptcies

If a taxpayer owes past due federal taxes that he or she cannot pay, bankruptcy may be an option.

- Before the taxpayer considers filing a bankruptcy, here are some things the taxpayer should know:
  - The taxpayer must file all required tax returns for tax periods ending within four years of the bankruptcy filing.
  - During the bankruptcy the taxpayer must continue to file, or get an extension of time to file, all required returns.
  - During the bankruptcy case the taxpayer should pay all current taxes as they come due.
- Failure to file returns and/or pay current taxes during the bankruptcy may result in the case being dismissed.

When a taxpayer files a bankruptcy petition, bankruptcy's automatic stay goes into effect. The stay temporarily stops most types of collection actions, including all tax collection efforts for pre-bankruptcy taxes.

To obtain full protection of the automatic stay, the IRS must be notified of the bankruptcy filing. The court will notify the IRS of the bankruptcy filing if the taxpayer lists the IRS as a creditor in the bankruptcy schedules. However, if there is a tax sale scheduled or other action pending, the taxpayer should also provide the IRS with proof of the bankruptcy that he or she filed.

If the tax is dischargeable in the bankruptcy proceeding, and the taxpayer receives a discharge, the IRS will be permanently enjoined (stopped) from pursuing collection of the debt.

If the tax is not dischargeable, the IRS can continue collection efforts against the taxpayer and the exempt property as soon as the taxpayer receives a discharge.

However, sometimes there is property that the trustee is administering in the bankruptcy case that creditors, including the IRS, will likely receive in a bankruptcy distribution. In that situation, the IRS might abate, or temporarily stop collection efforts until it receives a distribution from the bankruptcy trustee.

## How Is the Transfer Pricing Penalty Applied?

Taxpayers can discharge (wipe out) debts for federal income taxes in Chapter 7 bankruptcy only if all of the following conditions are true:

The taxes are income taxes. Taxes other than income, such as payroll taxes or fraud penalties, can never be eliminated in bankruptcy.

The taxpayer did not commit fraud or willful evasion. If he or she filed a fraudulent tax return or otherwise willfully attempted to evade paying taxes, such as using a false Social Security number on the tax return, bankruptcy can't help.

The debt is at least three years old. To eliminate a tax debt, the tax return must have been originally due at least three years before the taxpayer filed for bankruptcy.

The taxpayer filed a tax return. The taxpayer must have filed a tax return for the debt he or she wishes to discharge at least two years before filing for bankruptcy. (In most courts, if the taxpayer files a late return (meaning the extensions have expired and the IRS filed a substitute return on their behalf), the taxpayer has not filed a "return" and cannot discharge the tax. In some courts, the taxpayer can discharge tax debt that is the subject of a late return as long as he or she meets the other criteria.)

The taxpayer passes the "240-day rule." The income tax debt must have been assessed by the IRS at least 240 days before the taxpayer files a bankruptcy petition or must not have been assessed yet. (This time limit may be extended if the IRS suspended collection activity because of an offer in compromise or a previous bankruptcy filing.)

**IRS Enforcement to Collect Unpaid Taxes**

If a taxpayer doesn't pay the tax in full when he or she files the tax return, he or she will receive a bill for the amount that is owed. This bill starts the collection process, which continues until the account is satisfied or until the IRS may no longer legally collect the tax; for example, when the time or period for collection expires.

The unpaid balance is subject to interest that compounds daily and a monthly late payment penalty.

If the taxpayer is not able to pay the balance in full immediately, the IRS may be able to offer the taxpayer a monthly installment agreement. Interest and late payment penalties will continue to accrue while the taxpayer makes installment payments.

If taxes are not paid timely, and the IRS is not notified why the taxes cannot be paid, the law requires that enforcement action be taken, which could include the following:

1. Filing a Notice of Federal Tax Lien
2. Issuing a Notice of Levy on salary and other income, bank accounts or property (legally seize property to satisfy the tax debt)
3. Assessing a Trust Fund Recovery Penalty for certain unpaid employment taxes
4. Offsetting a refund to which the taxpayer is entitled
5. Issuing a Summons to the taxpayer or third parties to secure information to prepare unfiled tax returns or determine the taxpayer's ability to pay

**Federal Tax Lien**

The federal tax lien gives the IRS a legal claim to all of the taxpayer's property for the amount of the tax liability. The federal tax lien arises when the tax liability has been assessed, a demand is made for its payment, and the taxpayer does not pay it.

A federal tax lien is the government's legal claim against a property when individuals neglect or fail to pay a tax debt. The lien protects the government's interest in all of the property, including real estate, personal property and financial assets.

**A federal tax lien exists after:**

**The IRS:**

Puts the balance due on the books (assesses the liability).

Sends the taxpayers a bill that explains how much they owe (Notice and Demand for Payment); and

**The taxpayers:**

Neglect or refuse to fully pay the debt in time.

The IRS will withdraw a Notice of Federal Tax Lien if the notice was filed while a bankruptcy automatic stay was in effect. The IRS may withdraw a Notice of Federal Tax Lien if the IRS determines:

1. The Notice was not filed according to IRS procedures
2. Individuals enter into an installment agreement to satisfy the liability unless the installment agreement provides otherwise
3. Withdrawal will allow individuals to pay their taxes more quickly or
4. Withdrawal is in the best interest, as determined by the National Taxpayer Advocate, and in the best interest of the government.

**How to Get Rid of a Lien**

Paying the tax debt - in full - is the best way to get rid of a federal tax lien. The IRS releases the lien within 30 days after the taxpayer has paid the tax debt.

When conditions are in the best interest of both the government and the taxpayer, other options for reducing the impact of a lien exist.

**Discharge of property** -A "discharge" removes the lien from specific property. There are several Internal Revenue Code (IRC) provisions that determine eligibility.

**Subordination** - "Subordination" does not remove the lien but allows other creditors to move ahead of the IRS, which may make it easier to get a loan or mortgage.

**Withdrawal** - A "withdrawal" removes the public Notice of Federal Tax Lien and assures that the IRS is not competing with other creditors for the property; however, the taxpayer is still liable for the amount due.

### How a Lien Affects Taxpayers

**Assets** — A lien attaches to all of the assets (such as property, securities, vehicles) and to future assets acquired during the duration of the lien.

**Credit** — Once the IRS files a Notice of Federal Tax Lien, it may limit the ability to get credit.

**Business** — The lien attaches to all business property and to all rights to business property, including accounts receivable.

**Bankruptcy** — If a taxpayer files for bankruptcy, the tax debt, lien, and Notice of Federal Tax Lien may continue after the bankruptcy.

### Releasing a Lien

The IRS issues a Certificate of Release of the Federal Tax Lien no later than 30 days after:

the taxpayer satisfies the tax liability (including tax, penalty, interest, and other additions) or the liability becomes legally unenforceable; or

The IRS accepts a bond guaranteeing payment of the debt.

After a Notice of Federal Tax Lien is filed, the IRS cannot issue a Certificate of Release of Federal Tax Lien until a condition for release, as noted above, is met. The taxpayer must also pay all fees that a recording office charges to file and release the lien.

### Notice To Levy

A levy is a legal seizure of the property to satisfy a tax debt. Levies are different from liens. A lien is a legal claim against property to secure payment of the tax debt, while a levy actually takes the property to satisfy the tax debt.

The Internal Revenue Code (IRC) authorizes levies to collect delinquent tax. Any property or right to property that belongs to the taxpayer or on which there is a federal tax lien can be levied, unless the IRC exempts the property from levy.

### What actions must the Internal Revenue Service take before a levy can be issued?

The IRS will usually levy only after these three requirements are met:

- The IRS assessed the tax and sent the taxpayer a Notice and Demand for Payment (a tax bill).
- The taxpayer neglected or refused to pay the tax; and
- The IRS sent the taxpayer a Final Notice of Intent to Levy and Notice of Your

Right to A Hearing (levy notice) at least 30 days before the levy. The IRS may give the taxpayer this notice in person, leave it at the taxpayer's home or a usual place of business, or send it to the last known address by certified or registered mail, return receipt requested. Please note: if the IRS levies the state tax refund, the taxpayer may receive a Notice of Levy on Your State Tax Refund, Notice of Your Right to Hearing after the levy.

## When will the IRS issue a levy?

If a taxpayer does not pay his or her taxes (or make arrangements to settle a debt), and the IRS determines that a levy is the next appropriate action, the IRS may levy any property or right to property the taxpayer owns or have an interest in. For instance, the IRS could levy property owned by the taxpayer, but is held by someone else (such as the wages, retirement accounts, dividends, bank accounts, licenses, rental income, accounts receivables, the cash loan value of the life insurance, or commissions). Or the IRS could seize and sell property that the taxpayer holds (such as a car, boat or house).

## How Do I Get a Levy Released?

The IRS is required to release a levy if it determines that:
- The taxpayer paid the amount owed,
- The period for collection ended prior to the levy being issued,
- Releasing the levy will help the taxpayer to pay the taxes,
- The taxpayer enters into an Installment Agreement and the terms of the

agreement don't allow for the levy to continue,
- The levy creates an economic hardship, meaning the IRS has determined the levy prevents the taxpayer from meeting basic, reasonable living expenses, or
- The value of the property is more than the amount owed and releasing the levy will not hinder our ability to collect the amount owed.

## IRS Summons

### Who May be Summoned?

IRC 7602 permits a summons to be issued to:
- a person liable for tax,
- an officer or employee of such person,
- a person with possession, custody, or care of the business books of a person liable for tax, or
- any other person that the examiner deems necessary.

A summons may be issued to a political organization for the purpose of determining exempt status or tax liability. The EP/EO key district director must authorize such a summons before it is issued. IRM 7(10)22.2(2) provides that a political organization includes:
A. a political party.
B. a national, state or local committee of a political party; and
C. a campaign committee or other organization that accepts contributions or makes expenditures to influence the selection of any candidate for public office.

## Why Issue Summons?

The purposes for which the Service may issue summonses are as follows:
- To ascertain the correctness of any return.
- To prepare a return where none has been made.
- To determine the liability of a person for any internal revenue tax.
- To determine the liability at law or in equity of a transferee or fiduciary of a person in respect of any internal revenue tax.
- To collect any internal revenue tax liability.
- To inquire into any offense (civil or criminal) connected with the administration or enforcement of the internal revenue laws.

## Why Issue Summons?

A summons should only be issued when:
- The information required is vital to the investigation.
- the taxpayer or third-party summoner is unreasonably refusing to cooperate; and
- the information cannot be easily obtained from other sources.

## What May Be Summoned?

The examiner can use a summons to compel testimony and/or the production of relevant books, papers, records, or other data. The information, however, must already be in existence.

Original documents, not just copies, may be summoned. Also, a summons may request more than written materials. Examiners may summon computer tapes, video cassettes, handwriting examples, and any other type of information.

Where the information is stored on tapes or in a computer format, it may be necessary to summon information about the tape or computer system sufficient to access the information. Service computer specialists can help in crafting such summons requests.

**Taxpayer Collection Appeal Rights**

**Requesting An Appeal**

After considering an appeal and determining that Appeals is the place for the taxpayer, he or she may request an appeal by filing a written protest. Complete a protest and mail it to the IRS address on the letter that explains the appeal rights. Don't send the protest directly to the Office of Appeals; this will only delay the process and may prevent Appeals from considering the case.

Before sending the case to Appeals, the IRS Examination or Collection office that made a tax assessment or initiated collection action will consider the protest and attempt to resolve the disputed tax issues. If that office can't resolve these issues, they will forward the case to Appeals for consideration.

- When the taxpayer comes to Appeals, he or she may represent himself or herself or have a professional represent the taxpayer. The representative must be:
- An attorney
- A certified public accountant, or
- An enrolled agent authorized to practice before the IRS

**File a Protest**

The IRS requires a formal written protest to request an Appeals conference, unless the taxpayer qualifies under the Small Case Request procedures discussed below. For information on filing a formal written protest or a Small Case Request.

The taxpayer must send the formal written protest within the time limit specified in the letter that offers the right to appeal the proposed changes. Generally, the time limit is 30 days from the date of the letter.

**How to File a Small Case Request**

Taxpayers may submit a Small Case Request if the entire amount of additional tax and penalty proposed for each tax period is $25,000 or less. If a taxpayer is appealing the denial of an offer in compromise, the entire amount for each tax period includes total unpaid tax, penalty and interest due. Employee plans, exempt organizations, S corporations and partnerships are not eligible for Small Case Requests.
- Follow the instructions in the received letter
- Use Form 12203, Request for Appeals Review, the form referenced in the received letter to file the appeal or prepare a brief written statement.

**Appeal a Collection Decision**

In addition, if a taxpayer is appealing a collection decision, he or she should select the appeal procedure listed below that corresponds to the case for specific instructions to prepare the request for appeals. Remember, if the taxpayer wants to present the dispute to Appeals, he or she will need to mail it to the office that sent the decision letter.

- Collection Appeals Program (CAP)
- Collection Due Process (CDP)
- Offer in Compromise (OIC)
- Trust Fund Recovery Penalty (TFRP)

**Collection Appeals Program (CAP)**

Collection Appeals Program (CAP) is generally quick and available for a broad range of collection actions. However, taxpayers can't go to court if they disagree with the Appeals decision. They may go through the CAP process if they are involved in any of the following collection actions:

- Lien
- Levy
- Seizure
- Rejection of Installment Agreement
- Termination of Installment Agreement
- Modification of Installment Agreement
- Collection Appeals Program (CAP)

**CAP Procedures**

- If the only collection contact has been a notice or telephone call:
- Call the IRS telephone number shown on the notice
- Explain why the taxpayer disagrees and that he or she wants to appeal the decision
- Be prepared to offer a solution
- Before the taxpayer can start the appeals process with the Office of Appeals, he or she will need to first discuss a case with a Collection manager, unless the appeal involved a rejected,

proposed for modification, modified, proposed for termination or terminated installment agreement

**If a taxpayer has already been in contact with a revenue officer:**

- Call the revenue officer the taxpayer has been dealing with
- Explain why the taxpayer disagrees and that he or she wants to appeal the decision

- Be prepared to offer a solution
- Before the taxpayer can start the appeals process with the Office of Appeals, he or she will need to discuss the case with a Collection manager, unless the appeal involved a rejected, proposed for modification, modified, proposed for termination or terminated installment agreement
- Complete Form 9423, Collection Appeals Request
- Submit the completed Form 9423 to the revenue officer within 3 days of the conference with the Collection manager
- Collection Appeals Program (CAP)

**Collection Due Process (CDP)**

Taxpayers are entitled to a Collection Due Process (CDP) hearing with appeals if the IRS sends them a notice that states, they have the right to request a CDP hearing, such as:

- Notice of Federal Tax Lien Filing and Your Right to a Hearing Under IRC 6320
- Final Notice - Notice of Intent to Levy and Notice of Your Right to A Hearing

- Notice of Jeopardy Levy and Right of Appeal
- Notice of Levy on Your State Tax Refund – Notice of Your Right to a Hearing
- Post Levy Collection Due Process (CDP) Notice

## Collection Due

## Process

### CDP Procedures

- Taxpayers generally have 30 days from the date of the notice to timely request a CDP hearing
- Complete Form 12153, Request for a Collection Due Process or Equivalent Hearing (PDF)
- It's important to identify all the reasons for any disagreement
- Send the completed Form 12153 to the same address that is shown on the CDP Notice
- If the request is timely made, the taxpayer will be entitled to an Appeals hearing and to seek judicial review of that hearing with the Tax Court
- If the request is timely, IRS levy action is generally suspended against the taxpayer for the tax periods that he or she appealed
- If the request is not timely, the taxpayer is still entitled to request a CDP Equivalent Hearing with Appeals within the 1-year period described in the Form 12153. However, if the taxpayer still disagrees with the Appeals decision in the Equivalent Hearing, he or she has no right to judicial review by the Tax Court

### Offer in Compromise (OIC)

An Offer in Compromise (OIC) is an agreement between the taxpayer and the government that settles a tax liability for payment of less than the full amount owed. If a taxpayer received a letter notifying him or her that the offer was rejected, he or she has 30 days from the date on the letter to request an appeal of the decision.

## Trust Fund Recovery Penalty (TFRP)

This penalty can apply if the taxpayer is a person responsible for:
  A. Collecting or withholding
  B. Accounting for or
  C. Depositing or paying specified taxes

If the taxpayer willfully fails to do so, he or she can be held personally liable for a penalty equal to the full amount of the tax that was not paid, plus interest. This includes:
  A. Non-resident alien (NRA) withholding
  B. Employment taxes
  C. Excise taxes

This penalty can apply if the taxpayer is a person responsible for:
  A. An owner or officer of a corporation
  B. A partner
  C. A sole proprietor
  D. An employee of any form of business

A trustee or agent with authority over the funds of the business can also be held responsible for the penalty. The assessment of the trust fund recovery penalty is applicable to the following tax forms: CT-1, 720, 941, 943, 944, 945, 1042 and 8288.

- In addition to the steps outlined in the publication, when preparing the formal written protest or small case request:
- Enclose a copy of the Letter 1153, Proposed Trust Fund Recovery Penalty Notification
- Explain why the taxpayer don't believe he or she is responsible for the unpaid taxes or the reason he or she disagrees with the amount of the proposed assessment(s)
- Include a clear explanation of the duties and responsibilities
- Cite the law or authority, if any, on which the taxpayer is relying

Send the protest to the attention of the IRS officer whose name and address are listed in the received Letter 1153.

# Pop Quiz &Answer Sheet
# Taxpayer's Financial Situation

## POP QUIZ

Test your knowledge on *Taxpayer's Financial Situation* by answering the questions below. The answer sheet may be found at the end of the Pop Quiz.

### Question 1:

What is the maximum term for a streamlined installment agreement?

A. 36 months
B. 48 months
C. 60 months
D. 72 months

### Question 2:

Which form should individuals use to request a monthly installment agreement?

A. Form 1040
B. Form 433-F
C. Form 9465
D. Form 8821

## Question 3:

Under which condition are individuals eligible for a guaranteed installment agreement?

A. They owe more than $10,000
B. They have failed to file income tax returns for the past 5 tax years
C. They agree to pay the full amount within 5 years
D. They are financially unable to pay the liability in full when due

## Question 4:

What document must individuals complete if the IRS determines their account is currently not collectible due to financial hardship?

A. Form 1040
B. Form 433-F
C. Form 9465
D. Form 8821

## Question 5:

What happens when a taxpayer files for bankruptcy in terms of IRS collection actions?

A. The IRS can continue all collection actions
B. The IRS is permanently enjoined from collecting pre-bankruptcy taxes
C. The automatic stay temporarily stops most types of collection actions
D. The IRS will immediately release all liens

## Question 6:

Which type of tax cannot be discharged in bankruptcy?

A. Income taxes
B. Payroll taxes
C. Excise taxes
D. All of the above

## Question 7:

What is a federal tax lien?

A. A temporary stop to collection actions
B. A legal claim against the taxpayer's property for the amount of the tax liability
C. A notice that the IRS will audit the taxpayer
D. A penalty for underpayment of taxes

## Question 8:

Which of the following actions can the IRS take to collect unpaid taxes?

A. Filing a Notice of Federal Tax Lien
B. Issuing a Notice of Levy on salary and other income
C. Seizing property to satisfy the tax debt
D. All of the above

**Question 9:**

What must happen before the IRS issues a levy?

A. The taxpayer must refuse to file a tax return
B. The taxpayer must receive a Notice and Demand for Payment
C. The taxpayer must request an installment agreement
D. The taxpayer must have unpaid property taxes


**Question 10:**

Which form should be used to request a Collection Due Process (CDP) hearing?

A. Form 433-F
B. Form 9465
C. Form 12153
D. Form 2848

# Answer Sheet
# Taxpayer's Financial Situation

## Question 1:

- **Answer:** D. 72 months

- **Explanation:** The maximum term for a streamlined installment agreement is 72 months.

## Question 2:

- **Answer:** C. Form 9465

- **Explanation:** Individuals should use Form 9465 to request a monthly installment agreement.

## Question 3:

- **Answer:** D. They are financially unable to pay the liability in full when due

- **Explanation:** Individuals are eligible for a guaranteed installment agreement if they are financially unable to pay the liability in full when due and meet other conditions.

## Question 4:

- **Answer:** B. Form 433-F

- **Explanation:** Individuals may need to complete Form 433-F if the IRS determines their account is currently not collectible due to financial hardship.

## Question 5:

- **Answer:** C. The automatic stay temporarily stops most types of collection actions

- **Explanation:** When a taxpayer files for bankruptcy, the automatic stay temporarily stops most types of collection actions.

## Question 6:

- **Answer:** D. All of the above

- **Explanation:** Taxes other than income, such as payroll taxes or fraud penalties, can never be eliminated in bankruptcy.

## Question 7:

- **Answer:** B. A legal claim against the taxpayer's property for the amount of the tax liability

- **Explanation:** A federal tax lien is the government's legal claim against a taxpayer's property for the amount of the tax liability.

## Question 8:

- **Answer:** D. All of the above

- **Explanation:** The IRS can take various actions to collect unpaid taxes, including filing a Notice of Federal Tax Lien, issuing a Notice of Levy on salary and other income, and seizing property to satisfy the tax debt.

## Question 9:

- **Answer:** B. The taxpayer must receive a Notice and Demand for Payment

- **Explanation:** Before issuing a levy, the IRS must send the taxpayer a Notice and Demand for Payment and the taxpayer must neglect or refuse to pay the tax.

## Question 10:

- **Answer:** C. Form 12153

- **Explanation:** Taxpayers should use Form 12153 to request a Collection Due Process (CDP) hearing.

# Legal Authority & References

## Overview

The IRS's role is to help many compliant taxpayers with tax law, while ensuring that the minority who are unwilling to comply pay their fair share.

The IRS provides America's taxpayers top quality service by helping them understand and meet their tax responsibilities and enforce the law with integrity and fairness to all.

The IRS is organized to carry out the responsibilities of the secretary of the Treasury under section 7801 of the Internal Revenue Code. The President appoints the Secretary of the Treasury, and Congress passes tax laws that require taxpayers to comply.

## Legal Authority of The Internal Revenue Service

The U.S. Treasury Department, (which includes the Internal Revenue Service), is part of the executive branch of the U.S

## Legislative (Makes Laws)

The Legislative Branch consists of the House of Representatives and the Senate, which together form the United States Congress.

## Executive (Carries out laws)

The power of the Executive Branch is vested in the President of the United States, who also acts as head of state and Commander- in-Chief of the armed forces. The President is responsible for implementing and enforcing the laws written by Congress and, to that end, appoints the heads of the federal agencies, including the Cabinet.

### Judicial (Evaluates Laws)

Where the Executive and Legislative branches are elected by the people, members of the Judicial Branch are appointed by the President and confirmed by the Senate.
Federal courts enjoy the sole power to interpret the law, determine the constitutionality of the law, and apply it to individual cases.

### US Department of Treasury

The treasury executes currency circulation in the domestic fiscal system paying various government expenditures allocated in its budget.

### Internal Revenue Service

Collects taxes which it sends to the U.S. Department of Treasury and enforces tax law. The IRS administers the Internal Revenue Code enacted by Congress.

### Internal Revenue Code
The Internal Revenue Code is a comprehensive set of tax laws created by the Internal Revenue Service published in various volumes of the United States Statutes at Large, and separately as Title 26 of the United States Code.

**Internal Revenue Code (Substantial Authority)**

- There are various ways you and taxpayers can use to determine the basis for interpretation of current tax law and to establish precedents for the future. They include the following.
- Temporary and final treasure regulations
- Administrative rulings
- Private Letter rulings
- technical advice memoranda
- IRS information or press releases
- IRS notices
- IRS postings to the Internal Revenue Bulletin
- Court Cases
- Tax treaties
- Congressional intent

**Because many IRS publications are not updated yearly publication and form instructions are not included as "substantial authority".**

**Treasury Regulation**

The IRS, under the supervision of the Treasury Department, issues Treasury Regulations to provide guidance for new Internal Revenue Code provisions or other tax law provisions or to address issues that arise with respect to existing IRC sections.

Treasury Regulations interpret the IRC, set forth the IRS's position and give directions on complying with tax laws.

The three types of treasury regulations are:

1. Legislative regulations
2. Interpretive regulations
3. Procedural regulations

**Types of Treasury Regulations:**

**Legislative Regulations**

Legislative regulations are rules made by the government that have the same importance as the actual law. These regulations usually mention the specific law they are based on. It is important for these regulations to follow the requirements of the Administrative Procedure Act (APA), which means they must be shared with the public for feedback before they are finalized.

**Interpretive Regulations**

Interpretive regulations are rules that help clarify what the IRS thinks about different parts of the tax laws (IRC sections). These regulations are made by the IRS to interpret the language in the tax laws, even though the laws themselves don't specifically authorize them.

Sometimes, interpretive regulations can be questioned if they don't align with what Congress intended when making the laws. However, these regulations still hold significant weight and are considered important.

Unlike some other regulations, interpretive regulations don't have to go through the usual process of being shared with the public for feedback before they are finalized. They are exempt from the normal requirements of the Administrative Procedure Act that governs how regulations are made.

## Procedural Regulations

Procedural regulations are rules that explain how to do certain things, like filing tax returns or making choices. These regulations are usually binding and must be followed.

However, there is a specific set of procedural rules called the Statement of Procedural Rules, found in 26 CFR Part 601. These rules are considered more like guidelines than strict requirements. They provide instructions for how the IRS operates internally. The IRS Commissioner creates these rules without needing the Treasury Secretary's signature.

Even though they are not mandatory, the procedural rules are still important. They are published in the Federal Register, which gives them the same status as regular regulations. This means they have more authority than other IRS announcements that are not published in the Federal Register.

# CLASSIFICATION OF TREASURY REGULATIONS

| Level | Description | Issuance | Weight of authority |
|-------|-------------|----------|---------------------|
| Proposed | Provide insight to how the IRS is interpreting the law; allow practitioners to have input in the process. | Published in the Federal Register via a Notice of Proposed rulemaking. | Cannot rely on proposed regulation to support tax position or for planning purposes, unless IRS clearly states otherwise. |
| Temporary | Provide guidance until final regulations are adopted. Valid for no more than 3 years from date issued, generally. | Published via a Treasury Division | Highest authority issued by the Treasury Department. |
| Final | Interpret an IRC section and provide guidance for tax compliance and planning purposes. | Published via a Treasury Division | Cannot rely on proposed regulation to support tax position or for planning purposes unless IRS clearly states otherwise. |

# REVENUE RULINGS & PROCEDURES

## Revenue Ruling

A revenue ruling is an official interpretation by the IRS of the Internal Revenue Code, related statutes, tax treaties and regulations. It is the conclusion of the IRS on how the law is applied to a specific set of facts. Revenue rulings are published in the Internal Revenue Bulletin for the information of and guidance to taxpayers, IRS personnel and tax professionals. For example, a revenue ruling may hold that taxpayers can deduct certain automobile expenses.

## Revenue Procedure

A revenue procedure is an official statement of a procedure that affects the rights or duties of taxpayers or other members of the public under the Internal Revenue Code, related statutes, tax treaties and regulations and that should be a matter of public knowledge. It is also published in the Internal Revenue Bulletin. While a revenue ruling generally states an IRS position, a revenue procedure provides return filing or other instructions concerning an IRS position. For example, a revenue procedure might specify how those entitled to deduct certain automobile expenses should compute them by applying a certain mileage rate in lieu of calculating actual operating expenses.

## IRS WRITTEN DETERMINATIONS

### Three types of IRS Written Determinations
1. Taxpayer-specific rulings or determinations written memoranda furnished by the IRS

National Office in response to requests by taxpayers under published annual guidelines. See Rev. Proc. 2008-1 and Rev. Proc. 2008-4 for more information about these guidelines.
2. Technical advice memoranda (TAM) are written memoranda furnished by the National Office of the IRS upon request of a district director or chief appeals officer pursuant to annual review procedures.
3. Chief Counsel Advice (CCA) materials are written advice or instructions prepared by the Office of Chief Counsel and issued to field or service center employees of the IRS or Office of Chief Counsel. See the Chief Counsel Advice Training Materials for more information about CCAs

**Technical Advice Memorandum**

A request for a TAM (Technical Advice Memorandum) usually comes up when the IRS examines a taxpayer's return, considers a refund or credit claim, or deals with a specific matter related to a taxpayer. TAMs are only issued for completed transactions and offer guidance on how to apply tax laws, treaties, regulations, and previous rulings correctly.

The advice given in a TAM represents the final decision of the IRS, but it only applies to the particular issue and case mentioned in the memorandum. TAMs are typically made available to the public once any information that could reveal the taxpayer's identity has been removed.

**Example of a Technical Advice Memorandum (TAM):**

Sarah, a taxpayer, is engaged in a complex international business transaction. She seeks guidance from the IRS regarding the tax treatment of certain aspects of the transaction. Sarah submits a written request to the IRS, providing all the relevant details and facts.

The IRS reviews Sarah's request and issues a TAM in response to her specific situation. The TAM is a written statement that interprets and applies tax laws, treaties, regulations, revenue rulings, or other precedents to address the tax consequences of Sarah's transaction.

In the TAM, the IRS provides Sarah with technical advice on how to properly apply the tax laws to her unique circumstances. It offers guidance on the correct interpretation and application of tax rules to ensure compliance and accurate reporting.

The TAM serves as a final determination of the IRS's position with respect to the specific issue in Sarah's case. It provides Sarah with clarity and certainty regarding the tax treatment of her transaction.

It's important to note that TAMs are generally made public after removing any identifying information that could link them to the specific taxpayer involved. However, TAMs cannot be relied upon as binding precedent by other taxpayers or IRS personnel.

## PRIVATE LETTER RULING

A private letter ruling (PLR) is a written statement provided to a taxpayer that explains how tax laws apply to their specific situation. The purpose of a PLR is to give the taxpayer certainty about the tax consequences of a specific transaction before it takes place or before they file their tax return.

To obtain a PLR, the taxpayer must submit a written request to the IRS, describing the proposed transaction accurately and completely. If the taxpayer follows through with the transaction as described, the PLR is binding on the IRS and establishes the tax outcome.

However, it's important to note that other taxpayers and IRS personnel cannot rely on a PLR as a precedent or official guidance. Generally, PLRs become public, but any identifying information about the taxpayer is removed before their release.

**Example of a Private Letter Ruling (PLR):**

John is a taxpayer who is considering selling a piece of real estate. Before making the sale, John wants to know the tax consequences of the transaction. He submits a written request to the IRS, describing the details of the proposed sale, including the purchase price, cost basis, and any relevant factors.

The IRS reviews John's request and issues a PLR specifically addressing his situation. In the PLR, the IRS provides a written statement that interprets and applies the tax laws to John's specific facts. The PLR explains how the sale of the real estate will be treated for tax purposes, including any potential tax liabilities, deductions, or credits associated with the transaction.

John can rely on this PLR as a binding agreement with the IRS. It gives him certainty about the tax consequences of the real estate sale, allowing him to proceed with the transaction with confidence. However, it's important to note that this PLR is specific to John's situation and cannot be used as a precedent or relied upon by other taxpayers or IRS personnel.

**IRS NOTICES**

**The IRS sends notices and letters for the following reasons:**
1. Taxpayers have a balance due.
2. Taxpayers are due a larger or smaller refund.
3. The IRS has a question about the tax return.
4. The IRS needs to verify a taxpayer's identity.
5. The IRS needs additional information.
6. The IRS changed the return.
7. The IRS needs to notify the taxpayers of delays in processing the returns.

A notice is a public pronouncement that may contain guidance that involves substantive interpretations of the Internal Revenue Code or other provisions of the law. For example, notices can be used to relate what regulations will say in situations where the regulations may not be published in the immediate future.

## INTERNAL REVENUE MANUAL

The IRS Internal Revenue Manual is the official source of instructions to IRS personnel relating to the organization, administration, and operation of the IRS. The IRM contains directions IRS employees need to carry out their responsibilities in administering IRS obligations, such as detailed procedures for processing and examining tax returns.

Procedures set forth in the IRM are not mandatory and are not binding on the IRS. The provisions are not issued pursuant to a mandate or delegation of authority by Congress and do not have the effect of a rule of law. Nonetheless, IRM offers insights into IRS procedures, and

The IRM is the primary, official source of

"instructions to staff" that relate to the administration and operation of the IRS. It details the policies, delegations of authorities, procedures, instructions and guidelines for daily operations for all IRS organizations. The IRM ensures that employees have the approved policy and guidance they need to carry out their responsibilities in administering the tax laws or other agency obligations.

**IRS Publications and Forms**

The IRS disseminates information to both taxpayers and preparers through its official publications. For example, Publication 17 covers the general rules for filing a federal income tax return for individuals. Publication 17 supplements information contained in the tax form instruction booklet and explains the law in more detail, so it is an important document for taxpayers who prepare their own income tax returns.

Although the information in publications is drawn from the Internal Revenue Code, Treasury regulations, and other primary sources of authority, publications themselves are not considered to have substantial authority. Taxpayers and preparers may not rely on guidance issued by IRS publications to avoid accuracy related penalties.

In 2014, a U.S. Tax Court judge declared, "Taxpayers rely on IRS guidance at their own peril." Judge Joseph W. Nega ruled against a married couple who used guidance from an IRS publication as the basis for their case disputing penalties imposed after an IRA withdrawal. The judge wrote that IRS guidance was not "binding precedent" or "sufficient authority" to excuse the couple from penalties. The IRS later revised the publication at issue.

## What Are Tax Forms?

Income tax forms are the official government documents the IRS requires taxpayers to fill out when they file their taxes. Usually, the more complicated the finances are the more tax forms the taxpayers may need to fill out.

On top of the federal tax forms, many states and cities have their own tax forms taxpayers may need to complete. Often, the local tax forms are modeled after the federal forms.

You can download tax forms from many places, including the IRS website.

## What Are Tax Schedules?

Tax schedules are another type of tax form individuals may be required to prepare and submit with the tax return when they have certain types of income or deductions, that can include income from interest, the sale of property, or charitable contributions. Here's a list of common schedules:

1. Schedule A Tax Form – Report Itemized Deductions
2. Schedule B Tax Form – Interest & Dividend Income
3. Schedule C Tax Form – Self Employed Income
4. Schedule D Tax Form – Capital Gain or Losses
5. Schedule E Tax Form – Real Estate Gain or Losses
6. Schedule SE Tax Form – Self-employment Tax
7. Schedule K-1 – Business Tax Form

## Adjudicated Case Law

Often, taxpayers and tax preparers will disagree with the IRS's interpretation of the IRC. In these cases, it is up to the courts to determine Congressional intent or the constitutionality of the tax law or IRS position that is being challenged. There are many instances where tax laws are disputed or even overturned. Court decisions then serve as guidance for future tax decisions. In most instances, the IRS chooses whether to acquiesce to a court decision. This means that the IRS may decide to ignore the ruling of the court and continue with its regular policies regarding the litigated issue.

The IRS is not bound to change its regulations due to a loss in court. The only exception to this rule is the U.S. Supreme Court, whose decisions the IRS is obligated to follow.

The IRS does not announce acquiescence or non-acquiescence in every case. Sometimes its position is withheld. When it does announce its position, the IRS publishes its acquiescence or non-acquiescence in the Internal Revenue Bulletin. The IRS can retroactively revoke acquiescence to any case.

## FREEDOM OF INFORMATION ACT REQUEST

The Freedom of Information Act (FOIA), 5 U.S.C. 552, gives people the right to request access to records or information held by federal agencies. This law applies to records created or obtained by the agency and under its control at the time of the request. Agencies in the executive branch, including the Executive Office of the President and independent regulatory agencies, must follow the FOIA. However, state governments, courts, Congress, and private citizens are not subject to the FOIA.

The IRS is required to consider FOIA requests for its records, but it can withhold certain information under nine exemptions and three exclusions defined in the FOIA statute.

There are cases where certain IRS records can be processed using routine agency procedures without going through the FOIA process. This is outlined in the regulations found in 26 CFR 601.702(d). Using established agency procedures can often be a more efficient way to obtain IRS information for FOIA requests.

The FOIA was enacted in 1966 and established the right for people to access records held by the Executive Branch of the U.S. Government. Before the FOIA, the disclosure of federal agency records to the public was governed by the Administrative Procedure Act, which was more focused on withholding information rather than disclosure.

The FOIA sets guidelines for determining which records should be made available to the public and which can be withheld. It also provides remedies for those denied access to records, both through administrative processes and in the courts. Overall, the FOIA requires federal agencies to disclose information to the public to the fullest extent possible.

## TAXPAYER BILL OF RIGHTS

The Taxpayer Bill of Rights (TBOR) outlines the 10 fundamental rights taxpayers have when working with the Internal Revenue Service. The IRS wants every taxpayer to be aware of these rights in the event they need to work with the IRS on a personal tax matter.
The IRS continues to publicly highlight these 10 taxpayer rights to taxpayers. The agency also regularly reminds its employees about these

rights. The IRS expects employees to understand and apply taxpayer rights throughout every encounter with taxpayers.

## TAX AVOIDANCE VS. TAX EVASION

### Tax Avoidance vs Tax Evasion

There's nothing wrong with wanting to pay less in taxes. Where taxpayers can run into trouble is how they go about decreasing their tax bill. There are legitimate tax avoidance steps taxpayers can take to maximize their after-tax income.

But failing to pay or deliberately underpaying their taxes is tax evasion and it's illegal.

**Tax Avoidance** Minimizing of taxes Examples:

1. Taking legitimate tax deductions to minimize business expenses and lower the business tax bill.

2. Setting up a tax deferral plan such as an IRA, SEP-IRA, or 401(k) plan to delay taxes until a later date.

3. Taking tax credits for spending money for legitimate purposes, like taking a tax credit for giving the employees paid family leaves.

### Tax Evasion

1. Under-reporting income (claiming less income than actually received from a specific source, particularly cash income.

2. Not reporting an income source.

3. Providing false information about business income or expenses
4. Deliberately underpaying taxes owed.
5. Keeping two sets of books.
6. Making false entries in books and records.
7. Claiming personal expenses as business expenses.
8. Claiming false deductions without having documents to support them
9. Hiding or transferring assets or income
10. Not paying taxes

## TAXPAYER ADVOCATE SERVICES

The Taxpayer Advocate Service (TAS) is an independent organization within the IRS and is your voice at the IRS.

TAS helps taxpayers whose problems are causing financial difficulty. This includes businesses as well as individuals.

Taxpayers may be eligible for help by TAS if they have tried to resolve their tax problem through normal IRS channels and have gotten nowhere or believes an IRS procedure just isn't working as it should.

TAS service is always free.

There is one local taxpayer advocate office in every state, the District of Columbia, and Puerto Rico.

TAS also handles large-scale or systemic problems that affect many taxpayers.

# Pop Quiz & Answer Sheet
# Legal Authority &
# References

## POP QUIZ

Test your knowledge on the Legal *Authority &
References* by answering the questions below. The
answer sheet may be found at the end of the Pop
Quiz.

**Q1:** **It interprets the IRC, sets forth the
IRS' position and gives directions on
complying with tax laws.**
A.   Technical Advice Memorandum
B.   Legal Authority
C.   Treasury Regulations
D.   Private Letter Ruling

**Q2:** **What is the level of classification of
treasury regulations that provides
insight to how the IRS is interpreting
the law; allows practitioners to have
input in the rulemaking process?**
A.   Proposed
B.   Temporary
C.   Final
D.   None of the Above

**Q3:** **Which branch of government passes tax laws?**
A.   Judicial
B.   Legislative
C.   Executive
D.   The President

**Q4:** **Which treasury regulations have the highest level of authority?**

A. Interpretive Regulation
B. Procedural Regulation
C. Legislative Regulation
D. Revenue Regulation

**Q5:** **If a taxpayer has a specific question regarding tax law, they may request a:**

A. Technical Advice Memorandum
B. Private Letter Ruling
C. Examination
D. Commissioner Letter Ruling

**Q6:** **Which of the following is the official compilation of policies, delegated authorities, procedures, instructions, and guidelines relating to the organization, functions, administration, and operations of the IRS?**

A. Internal Revenue Code
B. Internal Revenue Manual
C. Congress
D. The Department of Treasury

**Q7:** **A Technical Advice Memorandum only relates to:**

A. A Public Ruling
B. A Specific Case and Taxpayer
C. IRS Written Determinations
D. IRS Publications

**Q8:** **IRS records are subject to which of the following:**

A. To change its interpretation of the tax law due to a loss in court

B. To publish its acquiescence or nonacquiescence

C. Freedom of Information Act Requests

D. To Change its decision due to loss in a county court

**Q9:** **The IRS established the Taxpayer Bill of Rights to:**

A. Provide great customer service

B. To make it easier to examine or audit taxpayers

C. To better communicate to taxpayers their statutory and administrative protections

D. To detail IRS publication

**Q10:** **The taxpayer advocate service is:**

A. A local franchise office that prepares taxes for a fee

B. An independent organization within the IRS to help taxpayers resolve problems with the IRS

C. An organization in Washington DC where audits and examinations are conducted

D. All of the above

# Answer Sheet
# Legal Authority &
# References

## Question 1:

- **Answer:** C. Treasury Regulations

- **Explanation:** Treasury Regulations interpret the Internal Revenue Code (IRC), set forth the IRS's position, and provide directions on complying with tax laws.

## Question 2:

- **Answer:** A. Proposed

- **Explanation:** Proposed Treasury Regulations provide insight into how the IRS is interpreting the law and allow practitioners to have input during the rulemaking process.

## Question 3:

- **Answer:** B. Legislative

- **Explanation:** The Legislative branch of government, specifically Congress, passes tax laws.

## Question 4:

- **Answer:** C. Legislative Regulation

- **Explanation:** Legislative Regulations have the highest level of authority because they are issued under a specific grant of authority by Congress to prescribe the operation of a tax law.

## Question 5:

- **Answer:** B. Private Letter Ruling
- **Explanation:** A Private Letter Ruling is a written decision by the IRS in response to a taxpayer's specific inquiry about how the tax law applies to their particular set of facts.

## Question 6:

- **Answer:** B. Internal Revenue Manual
- **Explanation:** The Internal Revenue Manual is the official compilation of policies, procedures, instructions, and guidelines relating to the organization, functions, administration, and operations of the IRS.

## Question 7:

- **Answer:** B. A Specific Case and Taxpayer
- **Explanation:** A Technical Advice Memorandum (TAM) relates only to a specific case and taxpayer, providing guidance on the application of tax laws to the taxpayer's specific facts.

**Question 8:**

- **Answer:** C. Freedom of Information Act Requests

- **Explanation:** IRS records are subject to Freedom of Information Act (FOIA) Requests, which allows the public to request access to federal agency records or information.

**Question 9:**

- **Answer:** C. To better communicate to taxpayers their statutory and administrative protections

- **Explanation:** The Taxpayer Bill of Rights was established to better communicate to taxpayers their statutory and administrative protections.

**Question 10:**

- **Answer:** B. An independent organization within the IRS to help taxpayers resolve problems with the IRS

- **Explanation:** The Taxpayer Advocate Service is an independent organization within the IRS that helps taxpayers resolve problems with the IRS.

# Representing a Taxpayer in Audits

## Overview

An IRS audit is a review/examination of an organization's or individual's accounts and financial information to ensure information is reported correctly according to the tax laws and to verify the reported amount of tax is correct.

Selecting a return for examination does not always suggest that the taxpayer has either made an error or been dishonest. In fact, some examinations result in a refund to the taxpayer or acceptance of the return without change.

The overwhelming majority of taxpayers file returns and make payments timely and accurately. Taxpayers have a right to expect fair and efficient tax administration from the IRS, including verification that taxes are correctly reported and paid with enforcement actions against those who fail to comply voluntarily.

## How Returns Are Selected for Examination

The IRS selects returns using a variety of methods, including:

1. **Potential participants in abusive tax avoidance transactions** – Some returns are selected based on information obtained by the IRS through efforts to identify promoters and participants of abusive tax avoidance transactions.

Examples include information received from "John Doe" summonses issued to credit card companies and businesses and participant lists from promoters ordered by the courts to be turned over to the IRS.

2. **Computer Scoring** – Some returns are selected for examination on the basis of computer scoring. Computer programs give each return numeric "scores". The Discriminant Function System (DIF) score rates the potential for change, based on past IRS experience with similar returns. The Unreported Income DIF (UIDIF) score rates the return for the potential of unreported income. IRS personnel screen the highest-scoring returns, selecting some for audit and identifying the items on these returns that are most likely to need review.

3. **Large Corporations** – The IRS examines many large corporate returns annually.

4. **Information Matching** – Some returns are examined because payer reports, such as Forms W-2 from employers or Form 1099 interest statements from banks, do not match the income reported on the tax return.

5. **Related Examinations** – Returns may be selected for audit when they involve issues or transactions with other taxpayers, such as business partners or investors, whose returns were selected for examination.

6. **Other** – Area offices may identify returns for examination in connection with local compliance projects. These projects require higher level

management approval and deal with areas such as local compliance initiatives, return preparers or specific market segments.

## Types of Audits

IRS employees conduct examinations or audits in one of two ways.

1. **Correspondence Examinations**

Correspondence examinations are performed at IRS campus locations by tax examiners. The IRS currently employs 969 tax examiners conducting correspondence examinations of simple individual Form 1040 returns. Generally, the questionable issues are EITC, additional child tax credit, American opportunity tax credit, medical expenses, contributions, taxes, or employee business expenses. Tax examiners receive training on these issues but are not required to have accounting skills. An additional 144 tax examiners conduct correspondence examinations of non-resident alien returns (Form 1040NR) focusing generally on withholding.

Correspondence examinations are less burdensome for taxpayers than in-person audits as they mail in their documentation and don't have to travel in or take a day off from work to visit an IRS office. They are also the most efficient use of IRS' examination resources with a correspondence examination costing the IRS approximately $150. In FY 2018, the IRS conducted 75% of examinations by correspondence.

2. **Face-to-Face Examinations**

Tax Compliance Officers (TCOs), conduct face-to-face examinations in IRS offices (sometimes called an "office audit"). The IRS currently employs 572 TCOs. TCOs receive more training than tax examiners and have some accounting training. An audit by a TCO generally requires an in-office interview of the taxpayer but doesn't require an on-site inspection of the taxpayer's books, records, or assets. The types of issues selected for an office audit are income from tips, pensions, annuities, rents, fellowships, scholarships, royalties, and income not subject to withholding; deductions for business related expenses; deductions for bad debts; determinations of basis of property; capital gain versus ordinary income determinations; and complex miscellaneous itemized deductions such as casualty and theft losses.

The most complex returns, which are certain individual, corporate, and partnership returns, are audited by a Revenue Agent (RA) at the taxpayer's place of business.
Revenue Agents are our most highly trained and experienced employees with substantial accounting skills and are GS-9, 11, 12, 13, and 14. The IRS currently employs 6,463 RAs. Their skills are required due to the complex business transactions of the taxpayer, more voluminous records, and extensive time required to complete the audit.

In addition, the issues involved in a RA audit may require assistance from a specialist, such as an engineer, economist, or appraiser. Since these are the costliest examinations conducted by the IRS, RAs are directed to the most egregious noncompliance areas. These include high income, high wealth taxpayers, cash intensive businesses, transfer pricing, executive compensation, research and development credits, crypto currencies, partnerships and flow through entities, micro captives, offshore transactions, and syndicated conservation easements.

## Taxpayer Examination Rights and Obligations

The IRS trains its employees to explain and protect taxpayers' rights throughout their contacts with taxpayers. These rights include:

    A. A right to professional and courteous treatment by IRS employees.

    B. A right to privacy and confidentiality about tax matters.

    C. A right to know why the IRS is asking for information, how the IRS will use it and what will happen if the requested information is not provided.

    D. A right to representation, by oneself or an authorized representative.

    E. A right to appeal disagreements, both within the IRS and before the courts.

## The Taxpayer's Representative

Individuals have the right to retain an authorized representative of their choice to represent them in the dealings with the IRS.

## What individuals can expect:

Individuals may select a person, such as an attorney, certified public accountant or enrolled agent to represent them in an interview with the IRS. They do not have to attend with their representative unless the IRS formally summons them to appear.

In most situations, the IRS must suspend an interview if they request to consult with a representative, such as an attorney,

CPA or enrolled agent.

Individuals may have any attorney, CPA, enrolled agent, enrolled actuary, or any other person allowed to represent taxpayers before the IRS submits a written power of attorney to represent them. The person must not be disbarred or suspended from practice before the IRS.

If the income is below a certain level, individuals may ask a Low-Income Taxpayer Clinic to represent them in their tax dispute before the IRS or a federal court. The services are free or for a minimal fee. Many LITCs offer services in languages other than English. Although LITCs get partial funding from the IRS, LITCs, their employees and their volunteers are independent of the IRS.

**Audit Location and Procedures**

An examination usually begins when the taxpayers are notified that their return has been selected. The IRS will tell them which records they will need. The examination can proceed more easily if they gather the records before any interview. Any proposed changes to their return will be explained to them or the authorized representative. It is important that the taxpayers understand the reasons for any proposed changes. They should not hesitate to ask about anything that is unclear to them.

The IRS must follow the tax laws set forth by Congress in the Internal Revenue Code. The IRS also follows Treasury Regulations, other rules, and procedures that were written to administer the tax laws and court decisions. However, the IRS can lose cases that involve taxpayers with the same issue and still apply its interpretation of the law to the situation.

Most taxpayers agree to changes proposed by examiners, and the examinations are closed at this level. If the taxpayers do not agree, they can appeal any proposed change by following the procedures provided to them by the IRS.
Every audit focuses on certain aspects of a return, but the kinds of records the IRS requests will most likely be on the following list. No record can stand on its own.
Taxpayers must include the circumstances surrounding any document they send. Remember, only send copies.

**Receipts** – Present these by date with notes on what they were for and how the receipt relates to the business. In addition to providing the dollars paid or received for a service or product, certain kinds of receipts can prove mileage.

**Bills** – Include the name of the person or organization receiving payment, the type of service and the dates they are paid.

**Canceled checks** – Group these with copies of the bills they paid and any applicable employer reimbursement.

**Legal papers** – Include a description of what the case was about, when it happened and how it relates to the business, credit or deduction. Examples include:
- Divorce settlements including custody agreements
- Criminal or civil defense papers
- Property acquisition

- Tax preparation or advice

**Loan agreements** – Include a copy of the original loan with the following:
- Names of the borrowers
- Location of the property
- Financial institution making the loan
- Amount borrowed
- Terms (the number of months to pay)
- Settlement sheet
- If the loan was from an institution, include an end of tax year statement indicating interest paid
- If the loan was not from an institution, provide a statement from the payee indicating the interest paid that year as well as the payee's address and Social Security number
- Provide a breakdown of how the money are being used

**Logs or diaries** – These might show the dates and locations of the taxpayers' travel as well as the business purpose and mileage. These might also show gambling winnings and losses as well as dates and locations. These might also show job-hunting activity and expenses.

**Tickets** – Label travel tickets with the business purpose for the trip and group them with other receipts from the same trip. Lottery tickets help provide proof of profit or loss.

**Medical and Dental records**
- Medical savings account statements
- A copy of a handbook or other statements showing benefit and reimbursement policies
- Physician statements
- Capital improvement records for medical purposes including appraisals of the property

before and after the improvements
- Contract for attendant care

**Theft or loss documents**
- Insurance reports detailing the nature of the loss or damage
- If not insured, copies of fire department or police reports on the loss, theft or accident
- Photos or video showing the extent of the damage (if available)
- Appraisal from a qualified adjustor showing fair market value of the property before and after as well as an estimate of the damage
- Brief explanation of the loss

**Employment documents** – These might include uniform policies or dress codes, continued education requirements, W-2 reimbursement statements or policies.

**Schedule K-1** – These are used to report each shareholder's share of income, losses, deductions and credits when an S corporation files its annual tax return.

## Notice Of IRS Contact of Third Parties

The IRS must give taxpayers reasonable notice before contacting other persons about the tax matters. Taxpayers must be given reasonable notice in advance that, in examining or collecting the tax liability, the IRS may contact third parties such as their neighbors, banks, employers, or employees. The IRS must also give notice of specific contacts by providing the taxpayers with a record of persons contacted on both a periodic basis and upon their request.

**This provision does not apply:**
- To any pending criminal investigation,
- When providing notice would jeopardize collection of any tax liability,
- Where providing notice may result in reprisal against any person, or
- When taxpayers authorized the contact.

## REVENUE AGENT REPORTS (RAR)

Revenue Agent Reports (RARs) should contain all the information necessary to ensure a clear understanding of the adjustments and demonstrate how the tax liability was computed. Based upon the importance of the RAR, examiners should take all necessary steps to ensure report accuracy. Workpapers are the written records kept by the examiner that provide the principal support for the RAR and document the procedures applied, tests performed, information obtained, and the conclusions reached in the examination. They should include all the information necessary to conduct the examination and support the audit results.

A regular agreed report (Form 4549) may contain up to three tax years. Agreed RARs require the taxpayer's signature and include a statement that the report is subject to the acceptance of the Area Director, Area Manager, Specialty Tax.

Generally, the report forms for unagreed cases are identical to the report forms for agreed cases. Some exceptions include examinations involving non-taxable returns. All unagreed cases require written comment regarding:

A. The Team Manager's involvement in the examination
B. The validity of the issues involved, and
C. A statement that a closing conference was or was not held with the taxpayer. Form 886-A is

the written explanation of adjustments in all unagreed cases. If an adjustment involves a detailed computation, a worksheet will be attached.

## Audit Determinations

**An audit can be concluded in three ways:**
1. **No change:** an audit in which individuals have substantiated all of the items being reviewed and results in no changes.
2. **Agreed:** an audit where the IRS proposed changes and individuals understand and agree with the changes.
3. **Disagreed**: an audit where the IRS has proposed changes and individuals understand but disagree with the changes.

## Audit Reconsideration

An audit reconsideration is the process the IRS uses to re-evaluate the results of a prior audit where additional tax was assessed and remains unpaid, or a tax credit was reversed. If the taxpayer disagrees with the original determination, he/she must provide new information for the audited issue(s) that was not previously considered during the original examination. It is also the process the IRS uses when the taxpayer contests a substitute for return (SFR) determination by filing an original delinquent return or when there is a n IRS computational or processing error in assessing the tax.

Some reasons for an audit reconsideration request:
- The taxpayer did not appear for the audit.

- The taxpayer moved and did not receive the correspondence from the IRS.
- The taxpayer has new documentation pertinent to the audited issue(s) to present.

**Audit Reconsiderations**

A taxpayer might request an audit reconsideration if:

1. The taxpayer disagrees with an audit assessment from an audit of his/her return.
2. The taxpayer disagrees with an assessment created under the authority of IRC 6020(b), Substitute for Return (SFR).
3. The taxpayer has been denied tax credits such as earned income credit (EITC) claimed, during prior examination.

**In order to request an audit reconsideration:**

1. The taxpayer must have filed a tax return.
2. The assessment remains unpaid, or the Service has reversed tax credits that the taxpayer is disputing.
3. The taxpayer must identify which adjustments he/she is disputing.
4. The taxpayer must provide new additional information for the audited issue(s) not considered during the original examination.
5. There was an IRS computational or processing error in assessing the tax.

**Repeat Examinations**

The IRS tries to avoid repeat examinations of the same items, but sometimes this happens.
If the tax return was examined for the same items in either of the 2 previous years and no change was

proposed to the tax liability, please contact the IRS as soon as possible to see if the examination should be discontinued.

# Pop Quiz & Answer Sheet Representing A Taxpayer in Audits/Examinations

## POP QUIZ

Test your knowledge on *Representing a Taxpayer in Audits/Examinations* by answering the questions below. The answer sheet may be found at the end of the Pop Quiz.

### Question 1:

Which of the following methods is NOT used by the IRS to select returns for examination?

A. Potential participants in abusive tax avoidance transactions
B. Computer Scoring
C. Information Matching
D. Small Corporations

### Question 2:

The IRS selects returns for examination using the following methods, except:

A. Computer Scoring – Some returns are selected for examination on the basis of computer scoring.
B. Related Examinations – Returns may be selected for audit when they involve issues or transactions with other taxpayers, such as business partners or investors, whose returns were selected for examination.
C. Information Matching – Some returns are examined because third party reports such as form W-2 or 1099 do not match the applicable amounts reported on the tax return.

D. Small Corporations – The IRS examines many small corporate returns annually.


## Question 3:

In an office audit, all of the following are correct, except:

A. Office audits are held at the taxpayer's place of business
B. Office audits are held at a local IRS office
C. An IRS examiner interviews and reviews the taxpayer's paperwork in-person
D. The taxpayer can choose to represent himself or have an enrolled practitioner represent them


## Question 4:

In some cases, the Revenue Agent may require assistance during an audit from the following specialists, except:

A. Engineer
B. Appraiser
C. Economist
D. Judge


## Question 5:

The IRS trains its employees to explain and protect taxpayers' rights throughout their contacts with taxpayers. These rights do not include:

A. A right to know why the IRS is asking for information, how the IRS will use it and what will happen if the requested information is not provided.
B. A right to representation, by oneself or an authorized representative.
C. A right to appeal disagreements, both within the IRS and

before the courts.
D. A right to object and cancel the examination process.


## Question 6:

All of the following are audit determinations, except:

A. No change
B. Unagreed
C. Agreed
D. Mutually Acceptable


## Question 7:

If a taxpayer refuses to produce requested documents, an examiner may issue a:

A. Request to the Tax Court
B. Summons
C. Notice of complaint to the District Director on the taxpayer
D. Power of Attorney and Declaration of Representative


## Question 8:

In an audit where the IRS proposes changes and the taxpayer understands but disagrees with the changes, all of the following are true, except:

A. A conference with the IRS manager may be requested for further review of the issues.
B. The taxpayer may request fast track mediation or an appeal.
C. A taxpayer has to file a written protest to request fast track mediation.
D. A taxpayer may choose to go to court and contest the IRS determination.

**Question 9:**

Which of the following should not be done when requesting an audit reconsideration?

A. The taxpayer must have filed a tax return.
B. The assessment is paid, or the IRS has not reversed tax credits that the taxpayer is disputing.
C. The taxpayer must identify which adjustments he/she is disputing.
D. The taxpayer must provide new additional information for the audited issue(s) not considered during the original examination.

**Question 10:**

The following are some reasons for an audit reconsideration request, except:

A. The taxpayer signed a document such as a closing agreement entered into under IRC §7121.
B. The taxpayer did not appear for the audit.
C. The taxpayer moved and did not receive the correspondence from the IRS.
D. The taxpayer has new documentation pertinent to the audited issue(s) to present.

# Answer Sheet
# Representing A Taxpayer in
# Audits/Examinations

## Question 1:

- **Answer:** D. Small Corporations

- **Explanation:** The IRS does not specifically select returns based on the size of the corporation. Instead, they use methods like identifying abusive tax avoidance transactions, computer scoring, and information matching.

## Question 2:

- **Answer:** D. Small Corporations – The IRS examines many small corporate returns annually.

- **Explanation:** The IRS does not specifically target small corporations for examination as a method. They select returns based on factors such as computer scoring, related examinations, and information matching.

## Question 3:

- **Answer:** A. Office audits are held at the taxpayer's place of business

- **Explanation:** Office audits are held at a local IRS office, not at the taxpayer's place of business. Field audits, however, can be held at the taxpayer's place of business.

## Question 4:

- **Answer:** D. Judge

- **Explanation:** Revenue Agents might require assistance from specialists like engineers, appraisers, or economists, but not judges, as judges are not part of the IRS audit process.

## Question 5:

- **Answer:** D. A right to object and cancel the examination process.

- **Explanation:** Taxpayers do not have the right to cancel the examination process but do have rights to know why information is being requested, representation, and appeal disagreements.

## Question 6:

- **Answer:** D. Mutually Acceptable

- **Explanation:** The three possible audit determinations are no change, unagreed, and agreed. "Mutually Acceptable" is not an official term used in audit determinations.

## Question 7:

- **Answer:** B. Summons

- **Explanation:** If a taxpayer refuses to produce requested documents, the IRS examiner may issue a summons to compel the taxpayer to provide the information.

## Question 8:

- **Answer:** C. A taxpayer has to file a written protest to request fast track mediation.

- **Explanation:** A written protest is not necessary for fast-track mediation, but it is required to request an appeal.

## Question 9:

- **Answer:** B. The assessment is paid, or the IRS has not reversed tax credits that the taxpayer is disputing.

- **Explanation:** For an audit reconsideration, the assessment must remain unpaid, or the IRS has reversed tax credits that the taxpayer is disputing.

## Question 10:

- **Answer:** A. The taxpayer signed a document such as a closing agreement entered into under IRC §7121.

- **Explanation:** If a taxpayer signed a closing agreement, they typically cannot request an audit reconsideration as they have already agreed to the terms and conditions set forth in the agreement.

# Representing a Taxpayer Before Appeals

## Overview

To decide if the taxpayers should appeal the tax dispute, consider the following. If they believe the:

1   IRS made an incorrect decision based on a misinterpretation of the law, check the publications discussing the issue(s)

2   IRS didn't properly apply the law due to a misunderstanding of the facts, be prepared to clarify and support the position

3   IRS is taking inappropriate collection action against the taxpayers or the offer in compromise was denied, and they disagree with that decision, taxpayers must be prepared to clarify and support their position

4   Facts used by the IRS are incorrect, then the taxpayers should have organized records or other evidence to support their position

Appeals is the administrative appeals office for the IRS. Taxpayers may appeal most IRS decisions with the local Appeals Office. The Appeals Office is separate from - and independent of - the IRS Office taking the action they disagree with. The Appeals Office is the only level of administrative appeal within the IRS. Conferences with Appeals Office personnel are held in an informal manner by correspondence, by telephone or at a personal conference.

In most instances, taxpayers may be eligible to take their case to court if they don't reach an agreement at the Appeals conference, or if they don't want to appeal the case to the IRS Office of Appeals.

**Appealing After an Examination**

If taxpayers don't agree with any or all of the IRS findings given to them, they may request a meeting or a telephone conference with the supervisor of the person who issued the findings.

If taxpayers still don't agree, they may appeal the case to the Appeals Office of IRS.

If taxpayers decide to do nothing and the case involves an examination of the income, estate, gift, and certain excise taxes or penalties, they will receive a formal Notice of Deficiency. The Notice of Deficiency allows them to go to the Tax Court and tells them the procedure to follow. If taxpayers do not go to the Tax Court, the IRS will send a bill for the amount due.

**THE 90-DAY LETTER (NOTICE OF DEFICIENCY)**

Taxpayers have 90 days from the date this notice is mailed to file a petition with the Tax Court (or 150 days if the notice is addressed to them outside the United States). The last date to file the petition will be entered on the notice of deficiency issued by the IRS.

If taxpayers don't file the petition within the 90-day period (or 150 days, as the case may be), the IRS will assess the proposed liability and send a bill. Taxpayers may also have the right to take the case to the Tax Court in some other situations, for example, following collection action by the IRS in certain cases.

## U.S. TAX COURT

If the disagreement with the IRS is over whether the taxpayers owe additional income tax, estate tax, gift tax, certain excise taxes or penalties related to these proposed liabilities, they can go to the United States Tax Court. (Other types of tax controversies, such as those involving some employment tax issues or manufacturers' excise taxes, cannot be heard by the Tax Court.)

Taxpayers can do this after the IRS issues a formal letter, stating the amounts that the IRS believes they owe. This letter is called a notice of deficiency

## U.S. TAX COURT SMALL TAX CASE PROCEDURE

If taxpayers dispute not more than $50,000 for any one tax year, there are simplified procedures. They can get information about these procedures and other matters from the Clerk of the Tax Court, 400 Second St. NW, Washington, DC 20217.

## DELAY TACTICS ARE PROHIBITED

**Frivolous Filing Penalty Caution:**
If the Tax Court determines that the case is intended primarily to cause a delay, or that the position is

frivolous or groundless, the Tax Court may award
a penalty of up to $25,000 to the United States in its
decision.

## TAXPAYER RIGHTS TO BRING CIVIL ACTION

The Taxpayer Bill of Rights is a cornerstone
document that highlights the 10 fundamental
rights taxpayers have when dealing with the Internal
Revenue Service.

It includes The Right to Challenge the IRS's Position and Be
Heard.

- Taxpayers have the right to raise
  objections and provide additional
  documentation in response to formal
  IRS actions or proposed actions, to
  expect that the IRS will consider their
  timely objections and documentation
  promptly and fairly, and to receive a
  response if the IRS does not agree with
  their position.

## RECOVERING LITIGATION COSTS

Taxpayers may be able to recover the reasonable
litigation and administrative costs if they are the
prevailing party, and if you meet the other
requirements.

Taxpayers must exhaust the administrative
remedies within the IRS to receive reasonable
litigation costs. They must not unreasonably delay
the administrative or court proceedings.
Administrative costs include costs incurred on or
after the date they receive the Appeals decision
letter, the date of the first letter of proposed
deficiency, or the date of the notice of deficiency,

whichever is earliest.

## Recovering Litigation Costs

Recoverable litigation or administrative costs may include:

1. Attorney fees that generally do not exceed $125 per hour. This amount will be indexed for a cost-of-living adjustment.
2. Reasonable amounts for court costs or any administrative fees or similar charges by the IRS.
3. Reasonable expenses of expert witnesses.
4. Reasonable costs of studies, analyses, tests, or engineering reports that are necessary to prepare your case.

# Pop Quiz & Answer Sheet
# Representing a Taxpayer Before Appeals

## POP QUIZ

Test your knowledge on *Representing a Taxpayer before Appeals* by answering the questions below. The answer sheet may be found at the end of the Pop Quiz.

**Q1:  An individual can appeal for a tax dispute if he/she believes that:**

A.  The IRS made an incorrect decision based on a misinterpretation of the law.

B.  The IRS didn't properly apply the law due to a misunderstanding of the facts.

C.  The IRS is taking inappropriate collection action or the offer in compromise was denied, and the decision is unacceptable.

D.  All of the Above

**Q2:  If a taxpayer does not respond to a 30-day letter, or if he cannot reach an agreement with an appeals officer, the IRS will send him a _____.**

A.  Notice of Demand for Payment

B.  Notice of Deficiency also known as the 90-day Letter

C.  Notice of Delinquency

D.  Notice of Willful Neglect

**Q3:** **How many days from the date the notice of deficiency is mailed, can a taxpayer file a petition with the Tax Court?**

A.  90 days (150 days if addressed to a taxpayer outside the United States)

B.  120 days (150 days if addressed to a taxpayer outside the United States)

C.  150 days (175 days if addressed to a taxpayer outside the United States)

D.  180 days (200 days if addressed to a taxpayer outside the United States)

**Q4:** **The following individuals can practice before the U.S. Tax Court, except:**

A.  A taxpayer can represent himself or herself

B.  Attorneys

C.  Enrolled Agents & CPAs

D.  Enrolled Agents & CPA's who have earned the special designation "Admitted to Practice, U.S. Tax Court"

**Q5:** **If the taxpayer intended to cause a delay, or that its position is frivolous or groundless, how much penalty can the Tax Court award?**

A.  $15,000

B.  $25,000

C.  $50,000

D.  $75,000

**Q6:** **Which of the following is not part of the inclusions of litigation or administrative cost when appealing to the IRS?**

A. Reasonable amounts for court costs or any administrative fees or similar charges by the IRS.

B. Reasonable expenses of expert witnesses.

C. Reasonable costs of studies, analyses, tests, or engineering reports that are necessary to prepare the case.

D. All of the above

**Q7:** **If a taxpayer chooses to appeal an examiner's decision he can contact:**

A. A Local Appeals Office

B. A Local IRS Office that conducted the examination

C. Both 1 & 2

D. None of the Above

**Q8:** **What is required in all cases to request an Appeals conference?**

A. A Letter of Declaration

B. 30 Day Letter

C. A Formal Written Request unless the taxpayer qualifies for the small case request procedure

D. A Letter of Protest

**Q9:** **The tax court has generally held that taxpayers who rely on software to justify errors on self-prepared returns are:**

A.  Not liable for §6662 accuracy-related penalty
B.  Liable for 50% §6662 accuracy-related penalty
C.  Liable for 90% §6662 accuracy-related penalty
D.  Liable for §6662 accuracy-related penalty

**Q10:** **Which of the following is correct about an IRS appeal, except:**

A.  The contested tax has to be paid first if a taxpayer opts for either IRS appeals or the US Tax court
B.  Appeals does not abate the interest on a tax liability, interest continues to accrue
C.  The taxpayer may bypass both IRS appeals and the Tax court and take his case to the US court of federal claims or to a US district court
D.  Taxpayers may appeal either formally or informally within the IRS appeals system

# Answer Sheet

# Representing a Taxpayer Before Appeals

## Question 1:

- **Answer:** D. All of the Above

- **Explanation:** An individual can appeal if they believe the IRS made an incorrect decision based on a misinterpretation of the law, did not properly apply the law due to a misunderstanding of the facts, or if they find the collection action or denial of an offer in compromise inappropriate.

## Question 2:

- **Answer:** B. Notice of Deficiency also known as the 90-day Letter

- **Explanation:** If a taxpayer does not respond to a 30-day letter or cannot reach an agreement, the IRS will issue a Notice of Deficiency, also known as a 90-day letter, which gives the taxpayer 90 days to file a petition with the Tax Court.

## Question 3:

- **Answer:** A. 90 days (150 days if addressed to a taxpayer outside the United States)

- **Explanation:** A taxpayer has 90 days from the date the notice of deficiency is mailed (150 days if addressed to a taxpayer outside the United States) to file a petition with the Tax Court.

## Question 4:

- **Answer:** C. Enrolled Agents & CPAs

- **Explanation:** Enrolled Agents and CPAs can represent taxpayers before the IRS but cannot practice before the U.S. Tax Court unless they have earned the special designation "Admitted to Practice, U.S. Tax Court."

## Question 5:

- **Answer:** B. $25,000

- **Explanation:** The Tax Court can award a penalty of up to $25,000 if it finds that the taxpayer intended to cause a delay or that their position is frivolous or groundless.

## Question 6:

- **Answer:** D. All of the above

- **Explanation:** All the mentioned costs (court costs, expert witness expenses, and costs for necessary studies, analyses, tests, or engineering reports) are part of the inclusions of litigation or administrative costs when appealing to the IRS.

## Question 7:

- **Answer:** C. Both 1 & 2

- **Explanation:** A taxpayer can contact either a Local Appeals Office or the Local IRS Office that conducted the examination to appeal an examiner's decision.

## Question 8:

- **Answer:** C. A Formal Written Request unless the taxpayer qualifies for the small case request procedure

- **Explanation:** To request an Appeals conference, a formal written request is required unless the taxpayer qualifies for the small case request procedure.

## Question 9:

- **Answer:** D. Liable for §6662 accuracy-related penalty

- **Explanation:** The tax court generally holds taxpayers liable for the §6662 accuracy-related penalty, even if errors are due to reliance on software for self-prepared returns.

## Question 10:

- **Answer:** A. The contested tax has to be paid first if a taxpayer opts for either IRS appeals or the US Tax court

- **Explanation:** The contested tax does not have to be paid first if a taxpayer opts for IRS appeals or the US Tax Court. Taxpayers can appeal without prepayment of the tax in these forums.

# The Filing Process

### Signing an Electronic Tax Return

As with an income tax return submitted to the IRS on paper, the taxpayer and paid tax return preparer must sign an electronic income tax return. Taxpayers must sign individual income tax returns electronically. There are currently two methods for signing individual income tax returns electronically.

Taxpayers must sign and date the Declaration of Taxpayer to authorize the origination of the electronic submission of the return to the IRS prior to the transmission of the return to IRS.

The Declaration of Taxpayer includes the taxpayers' declaration under penalties of perjury that the return is true, correct and complete, as well as the taxpayers' Consent to Disclosure.

The Consent to Disclosure authorizes the IRS to disclose information to the taxpayers' Providers.

Taxpayers authorize Intermediate Service Providers, Transmitters and EROs to receive from the IRS an acknowledgment of receipt or reason for rejection of the electronic return, the reason for any delay in processing the return or refund and the date of the refund.

Taxpayers must sign a new declaration if the

electronic return data on individual income tax returns is changed after taxpayers signed the Declaration of Taxpayer and the amounts differ by more than either $50 to "Total income" or "AGI," or $14 to "Total tax," "Federal income tax withheld," "Refund" or "Amount you owe."

**Electronic Signature Methods**

There are two methods of signing individual income tax returns with an electronic signature available for use by taxpayers.

Both the Self-Select PIN and Practitioner PIN methods allow taxpayers to use a Personal Identification Number (PIN) to sign the return and the Declaration of Taxpayer.

The Self-Select PIN method requires taxpayers to provide their prior year Adjusted Gross Income (AGI) amount or prior year PIN for use by the IRS to authenticate the taxpayers.

This method may be completely paperless if the taxpayers enter their own PINs directly into the electronic return record using keystrokes after reviewing the completed return.

Taxpayers may also authorize EROs to enter PINs on their behalf, in which case the taxpayers must review and sign a completed signature authorization form after reviewing the return.

The Practitioner PIN method does not require the taxpayer to provide their prior year AGI amount or prior year PIN. Instead, taxpayers must always sign a completed signature authorization form.

Taxpayers who use the Practitioner PIN method must sign the signature authorization form even if they enter their own PINs in the electronic return record using keystrokes after reviewing the completed return.

Regardless of the method of electronic signature used, taxpayers may enter their own PINs; EROs may select and enter the taxpayers' PINs; or the software may generate the taxpayers' PINs; in the electronic return. After reviewing the return, the taxpayers must agree by signing an IRS e-file Signature Authorization containing the PIN.

### IRS E-File Requirements

1. Preparers are required to use the e-file program if 11 or more Forms 1040/1041 are filed during a calendar year.
2. E-file providers can be a sole proprietorship, partnership, corporation or other entity.
3. The firm submits an e-file application, meets the eligibility criteria and must pass a suitability check before the IRS assigns an Electronic Filing Identification Number (EFIN).
4. Applicants accepted for participation in IRS e-file are Authorized IRS e-file Providers.

## ELECTRONIC RETURN ORIGINATORS

An Electronic Return Originator (ERO) originates the electronic submission of returns it either prepares or collects from taxpayers who want to e-file their returns.

An ERO originates the electronic submission of a return after the taxpayer authorizes the filing of the return via IRS e file.

The ERO must have either prepared the

return or collected it from a taxpayer. An

ERO originates the electronic submission

by:
- Electronically sending the return to a Transmitter that transmits the return to the IRS
- Directly transmitting the return to the IRS (must also have a Transmitter role)
- Providing a return to an Intermediate Service Provider for processing prior to transmission to the IRS.

The ERO must always identify the paid tax return preparer (if any) in the appropriate field of the electronic record of returns it originates.

The ERO must enter the paid preparer's identifying information (name, address, Employer Identification Number (EIN), when applicable, and Preparer Tax Identification Number (PTIN)).

EROs may either transmit returns directly to the IRS or arrange with another Provider to transmit the electronic return to the IRS.

## AUTHORIZED TRANSMITTER

Sends the electronic return data directly to the IRS.

Eros and reporting agents may apply to be transmitters and transmit return data themselves, or they may contract with an accepted third-party transmitter that can transmit the data for them.

A transmitter must have software and computers that allow it to interface with the IRS.

## ELECTRONIC SIGNATURE REQUIREMENTS

The taxpayer authorizes on Form 8879. Can be a handwritten signature.

The e-signature option is only available to taxpayers e-filing their tax returns through an ERO, who uses software that provides identity verification and e-signature.

To meet e-signature requirements, the ERO must be able to record the taxpayer's name, social security number, address and date of birth electronically for identity verification purposes.

The software the ERO chooses to use dictates the e-signature method used to sign the form. Regardless of the method used, the electronic record must be tamper-proof once it is e-signed. Some examples of methods used to capture an e-signature include:

A. A handwritten signature captured on an e-signature pad.
B. A handwritten signature, mark, or command input on a display screen using a

        stylus device.

C. A digitized image of a handwritten signature that is attached to an electronic record.

D. A typed name.

E. A shared secret such as a PIN, password, or secret code, used to sign the electronic record.

F. A digital signature.

G. A mark captured as a graphic.

## E-FILE REJECTIONS

Rejected electronic individual income tax return data can be corrected and retransmitted without new signatures or authorizations if changes do not differ from the amount on the original electronic return by more than $50 to "Total income" or "AGI," or more than $14 to "Total tax," "Federal income tax withheld," "Refund" or "Amount you owe."

The ERO must give taxpayers copies of the new electronic return data.

## PAPER RETURNS SUBMITTED AFTER AN E-FILE REJECTION

If the IRS rejects the electronic portion of a taxpayer's individual income tax return for processing, and the ERO cannot fix the reason for the rejection, the ERO must take reasonable steps to inform the taxpayer of the rejection within 24 hours.

When the ERO advises the taxpayer that it has not filed the return, the ERO must provide the taxpayer with the business rule(s) accompanied by an explanation. If the taxpayer chooses not to have the electronic portion of the return corrected and transmitted to the IRS, or if the IRS cannot accept the return for processing, the taxpayer must file a paper return.

To timely file the return, the taxpayer must file the per return by the later of the due date of the return or ten calendar days after the date of the e-file rejection.

Taxpayers should include an explanation in the paper return as to why they are filing the return after the due date.

## SAFEGUARDING IRS E-FILE

Shared responsibility of the IRS and Authorized IRS e-file Providers.

Providers must be diligent in recognizing and

preventing fraud and abuse in IRS e-file. Providers

must report fraud and abuse to the IRS

Providers must also cooperate with IRS investigations by making available to the IRS, upon request, information and documents related to returns with potential fraud or abuse.

Providers appoint an individual as a Responsible Official who is responsible for ensuring the firm meets IRS e-file rules and requirements.

### Entity Electronic Filing Requirements

C-Corporations and S-Corporations: Corporations

with $10 million or more in total assets and that file 250 or more returns a year are required to electronically file Form 1120, 1120F, and 1120S.

- The total number of returns is determined by aggregating all returns, regardless of type, that are required to be filed over the calendar year, including income tax returns, returns required under Section 6033 of the Internal Revenue Code, information returns, excise tax returns, and employment tax returns.

Partnerships: > 100 Partners

Employment Tax Returns: Available for Form 940 and 941 series, 943, 944, and 945.

Estates and Trusts: Required if the preparer files more than 11 or more 1040/1041 series returns.

## PAPER RETURNS

If e-file rejections cannot be resolved:

To be considered timely filed the paper return must be postmarked by the later of the due date of the return, including extensions, or 10 calendar days after the date the IRS last gives notification the return was rejected as long as:

1. The first transmission was made on or before the due date of the return (including extensions) and

2. The last transmission was made within 10 calendar days of the first transmission.

Follow the steps below to ensure that the paper return is identified as a rejected electronic return, and the taxpayer is given credit for the date of the first rejection within the 10-day transmission perfection period:

1. The taxpayer must call the IRS e-help Desk (1-866-255-0654) to advise that they have not been able to have their return accepted.

2. The taxpayer should prepare the paper return and include all of the following:

   A. An explanation of why the paper return is being filed after the due date
   B. A copy of the reject notification or A brief history of actions taken to correct the electronic return
   C. Write in red at the top of the first page of the paper return "REJECTED ELECTRONIC RETURN – [DATE]." The date will be the date of first rejection within the 10-day transmission perfection timeframe.
   D. The paper return must be signed by the taxpayer. The PIN that was used on the electronically filed return that was rejected may not be used as the signature on the paper return.

## FORM W-2 REQUIREMENTS FOR E-FILING

Employers filing 250 or more Forms W-2 must file electronically unless granted a waiver by the IRS. All employers are encouraged to file Forms W-2 electronically.

The due date is January 31.

## E-FILE ADVERTISING STANDARDS

Providers must not use improper or misleading advertising in relation to IRS e file, including the periods for refunds and tax refund-related products.

A Provider must not advertise that individual income tax returns may be electronically filed prior to the Provider's receipt of Forms W-2, W-2G and 1099-R.

Advertisements must not imply that the Provider does not need Forms W-2, W-2G and 1099-R, or that it can use pay stubs or other documentation of earnings to e-file individual income tax returns.

In using the Direct Deposit name and logo in advertisement, the Provider must use the name "Direct Deposit" with initial capital letters or all capital letters, use the logo/graphic for Direct Deposit whenever feasible and may change the color or size of the Direct Deposit logo/graphic when it uses it in advertising pieces.

## IDENTITY PROTECTION PINS

The IP PIN is a six-digit number assigned to eligible taxpayers to help prevent the misuse of their Social Security number on fraudulent federal income tax returns.

An IP PIN helps the IRS verify a taxpayer's

identity and accept their electronic or paper tax return. When individuals have an IP PIN, it prevents someone else from filing a tax return with an SSN. The IP PIN is a valuable tool against tax-related identity theft. An IP PIN is used only on Forms 1040.

**Things to know before applying:**

1. Individuals must pass a rigorous identity verification process.
2. Only the online process is available.
3. Spouses and dependents are eligible for an IP PIN if they can pass the identity proofing process.
4. An IP PIN is valid for a calendar year.
5. Individuals must obtain a new IP PIN each year.
6. The IP PIN tool is unavailable mid-November through mid-January each year.
7. Correct IP PINs must be entered on electronic and paper tax returns to avoid rejections and delays.

**Taxpayers eligible for an IP PIN if:**

IRS sent them a CP01A Notice containing their IP PIN

Individuals filed their federal tax return last year as a resident of Arizona, California, Colorado, Connecticut, Delaware, District of Columbia, Florida, Georgia, Illinois, Maryland, Michigan, Nevada, New Jersey, New Mexico, New York, North Carolina, Pennsylvania, Rhode Island, Texas, Washington
They received an IRS letter inviting them to 'opt-in' to get an IP PIN.

**How to Get an IP PIN**

Eligible taxpayers who want an IP PIN can go to www.irs.gov/ippin to access the Get an IP PIN tool. Taxpayers who do not already have an account, must register with the IRS.

Make sure the taxpayer has all the necessary identity verification items:

- Email address
- Social Security Number (SSN) or Individual Tax Identification Number (ITIN)
- Tax filing status and mailing address
- One financial account number linked to their name:
  - Credit card – last 8 digits (no American Express, debit or corporate cards) or
  - Student loan
  - Mortgage or home equity loan or
  - Home equity line of credit (HELOC) or
  - Auto loan
  - Mobile phone linked to their name (for faster registration) or ability to receive an activation code by

**Levels of Infraction**s - Categories of infractions of IRS e-file rules based on the seriousness of the infraction with specified sanctions associated with each level. Level One is the least serious, Level Two is moderately serious, and Level Three is the most serious.

**Verifying Taxpayer Identity and Taxpayer Identification Numbers (TINs)**

To safeguard IRS e-file from fraud and abuse, an

ERO should confirm identities and SSNs, Adopted Taxpayer Identification Numbers (ATINs) and Individual Taxpayer Identification Numbers (ITINs) of taxpayers, spouses and dependents listed on returns prepared by its firm.

To prevent filing returns with stolen identities, an ERO should ask taxpayers not known to them to provide two forms of identification (photo IDs are preferable) that include the taxpayer's name and current or recent address. Also, seeing Social Security cards, ITIN letters and other documents for taxpayers, spouses and dependents avoids including incorrect TINs on returns.

Providers should take care to ensure that they transcribe all TINs correctly.

The TIN entered in the Form W-2, Wage and Tax Statement, in the electronic return record must be identical to the TIN on the version provided by the taxpayer.

The TIN on the Form W-2 should be identical to the TIN on the electronic return unless otherwise allowed by the IRS.

The IRS requires taxpayers filing tax returns using an ITIN to include the TIN, usually an SSN, shown on Form W-2 from the employer in the electronic record of the Form W-2. This may create an identification number (ITIN/SSN) mismatch as taxpayers must use their correct ITIN as their identifying number in the individual income tax return.

The IRS e-file system can accept returns with this identification number mismatch.

EROs should enter the TIN/SSN in the electronic record of the Form W-2 provided to them by taxpayers. Software must require the manual key entry of the TIN as it appears on Form W-2 reporting wages for taxpayers with ITINs.

EROs should ascertain that the software they use does not auto-populate the ITIN in the Form-W-2 and if necessary, replace the ITIN with the SSN on the Form W-2 the taxpayer provided. Incorrect TINs, using the same TIN on more than one return or associating the wrong name with a TIN are some of the most common causes of rejected returns.

Additionally, Name Control and TINs identify taxpayers, spouses and dependents. A Name Control is the first four significant letters of an individual taxpayer's last name, or a business name as recorded by the Social Security Administration (SSA) or the IRS. Having the wrong Name Control in the electronic return record for a taxpayer's TIN contributes to a large portion of TIN related rejects.

The most common example for a return rejecting due to a mismatch between a taxpayer's TIN and Name Control involves newly married taxpayers. Typically, the taxpayer may file using a correct SSN along with the name used in the marriage, but the taxpayer has failed to update the records with the SSA to reflect a name change.

To minimize TIN related rejects, it is important to verify taxpayer TINs and Name Control information prior to submitting electronic return data to the IRS. Be Aware of Non-Standard Information Documents the IRS has identified questionable Forms W-2 as a key indicator of potentially abusive and fraudulent returns.

Be on the lookout for suspicious or altered Forms W-2, W-2G, 1099-R and forged or fabricated documents.

EROs must always enter the nonstandard form code in the electronic record of individual income tax returns for Forms W-2, W-2G or 1099- R that are altered, handwritten or typed. An alteration includes any pen-and-ink change. Providers must never alter the information after the taxpayer has given the forms to them.

Providers should report questionable Forms W-2 if they see or become aware of them.

**Be Careful with Addresses**

Addresses on Forms W-2, W-2G or 1099-R; Schedule C or C-EZ; or on other tax forms supplied by the taxpayer that differ from the taxpayer's current address must be input into the electronic record of the return.

Providers must input addresses that differ from the taxpayer's current address even if the addresses are old or if the taxpayer has moved. EROs should inform taxpayers that, when the return is processed, the IRS uses the address on the first page of the return to update the taxpayer's address of record.

The IRS uses a taxpayer's address of record for various notices that it is required to send to a taxpayer's "last known address" under the Internal Revenue Code and for refunds of overpayments of tax (unless otherwise specifically directed by taxpayers, such as by Direct Deposit).

Providers must never put their address in fields reserved for taxpayers' addresses in the electronic return record or on Form 8453, U.S. Individual Income Tax Transmittal for an IRS e-file Return. The only exceptions are if the Provider is the taxpayer or the power of attorney for the taxpayer for the tax return.

# Pop Quiz & Answer Sheet
# The Filing Process

## POP QUIZ

Test your knowledge on *The Filing Process* by answering the questions below. The answer sheet may be found at the end of the Pop Quiz.

**Question 1:**

**Which of the following must a taxpayer do to authorize the origination of an electronic submission of their tax return to the IRS?**

A. Sign a waiver form
B. Sign and date the Declaration of Taxpayer
C. Provide only a verbal consent
D. Provide their Social Security Number

**Question 2:**

**Which method requires taxpayers to provide their prior year Adjusted Gross Income (AGI) amount or prior year PIN for IRS authentication?**

A. Practitioner PIN method
B. Self-Select PIN method
C. Digital Signature method
D. None of the above

**Question 3:**

**Which form must taxpayers sign if the electronic return data is changed and the amounts differ by more than $50 to "Total income" or "AGI," or $14 to "Total tax," "Federal income tax withheld," "Refund," or "Amount you owe"?**

A. Form 8879
B. Form 8453
C. Declaration of Taxpayer
D. Form 1040

**Question 4:**

**Who is responsible for ensuring that the firm meets IRS e-file rules and requirements?**

A. The taxpayer
B. The software provider
C. The Responsible Official appointed by the Provider
D. The IRS

**Question 5:**

**Which of the following is a requirement for EROs when using the e-signature method?**

A. Recording the taxpayer's name and address only
B. Recording the taxpayer's name, social security number, address, and date of birth
C. Recording the taxpayer's phone number
D. Recording only the taxpayer's consent

**Question 6:**

**Which taxpayers are required to file their returns electronically if they file 250 or more returns in a year?**

A. Only individual taxpayers
B. C-Corporations and S-Corporations with $10 million or more in total assets
C. Partnerships with fewer than 100 partners
D. Small businesses with fewer than 10 employees

**Question 7:**

**What should an ERO do if an electronic return is rejected and cannot be corrected?**

A. File the return electronically again without changes
B. Inform the taxpayer of the rejection within 24 hours
C. Discard the return
D. Submit a paper return immediately without informing the taxpayer

**Question 8:**

**What must be included in a paper return that is filed after an e-file rejection to ensure it is considered timely filed?**

A. Only the tax forms
B. A handwritten note
C. An explanation of why the paper return is being filed after the due date and a copy of the reject notification
D. The taxpayer's previous year's tax return

## Question 9:

**Which identity protection measure is assigned to eligible taxpayers to prevent the misuse of their Social Security number on fraudulent federal income tax returns?**

A. EFIN
B. AGI
C. IP PIN
D. TIN

## Question 10:

**What should providers do to safeguard IRS e-file from fraud and abuse?**

A. Confirm identities and TINs of taxpayers
B. Submit returns without verifying information
C. Allow taxpayers to file using any name they choose
D. Disregard any suspicious activity

# Answer Sheet
# The Filing
# Process

## Question 1:

- **Answer:** B. Sign and date the Declaration of Taxpayer

- **Explanation:** Taxpayers must sign and date the Declaration of Taxpayer to authorize the origination of the electronic submission of the return to the IRS prior to the transmission of the return.

## Question 2:

- **Answer:** B. Self-Select PIN method

- **Explanation:** The Self-Select PIN method requires taxpayers to provide their prior year AGI amount or prior year PIN for use by the IRS to authenticate the taxpayers.

## Question 3:

- **Answer:** C. Declaration of Taxpayer

- **Explanation:** Taxpayers must sign a new Declaration of Taxpayer if the electronic return data on individual income tax returns is changed and the amounts differ by more than $50 to "Total income" or "AGI," or $14 to "Total tax," "Federal income tax withheld," "Refund," or "Amount you owe."

## Question 4:

- **Answer:** C. The Responsible Official appointed by the Provider

- **Explanation:** Providers appoint an individual as a Responsible Official who is responsible for ensuring the firm meets IRS e-file rules and requirements.

## Question 5:

- **Answer:** B. Recording the taxpayer's name, social security number, address, and date of birth

- **Explanation:** To meet e-signature requirements, the ERO must be able to record the taxpayer's name, social security number, address, and date of birth electronically for identity verification purposes.

## Question 6:

- **Answer:** B. C-Corporations and S-Corporations with $10 million or more in total assets

- **Explanation:** C-Corporations and S-Corporations with $10 million or more in total assets and that file 250 or more returns a year are required to electronically file Form 1120, 1120F, and 1120S.

## Question 7:

- **Answer:** B. Inform the taxpayer of the rejection within 24 hours

- **Explanation:** If the IRS rejects the electronic portion of a taxpayer's individual income tax return for processing, and the

ERO cannot fix the reason for the rejection, the ERO must take reasonable steps to inform the taxpayer of the rejection within 24 hours.

## Question 8:

- **Answer:** C. An explanation of why the paper return is being filed after the due date and a copy of the reject notification

- **Explanation:** To ensure that the paper return is identified as a rejected electronic return and the taxpayer is given credit for the date of the first rejection within the 10-day transmission perfection period, the taxpayer should include an explanation of why the paper return is being filed after the due date and a copy of the reject notification.

## Question 9:

- **Answer:** C. IP PIN

- **Explanation:** The IP PIN (Identity Protection Personal Identification Number) is a six-digit number assigned to eligible taxpayers to help prevent the misuse of their Social Security number on fraudulent federal income tax returns.

## Question 10:

- **Answer:** A. Confirm identities and TINs of taxpayers

- **Explanation:** To safeguard IRS e-file from fraud and abuse, providers should confirm the identities and TINs (Taxpayer Identification Numbers) of taxpayers, spouses, and dependents listed on returns prepared by their firm.

# Due Diligence & Identity Theft

## Overview

Paid preparers of federal income tax returns or claims involving the earned income credit (EIC), child tax credit (CTC)/additional child tax credit (ACTC), credit for other dependents (ODC), American opportunity tax credit (AOTC), and/or head of household (HOH) filing status must meet due diligence requirements in determining the taxpayer's eligibility for, and the amount of, the credit and filing status.

Paid preparers will have complied with the due diligence requirements set forth in Treasury Regulations for the EIC, the CTC/ACTC/ODC, the AOTC, and/or HOH filing status claimed on a return or claim for refund if all of the following is done:

- Meet the knowledge requirement by interviewing the taxpayer, asking adequate questions, contemporaneously documenting the questions and the taxpayer's responses on the return or in notes, reviewing adequate information to determine if the taxpayer is eligible to claim the credit(s) and/or HOH filing status, and to compute the amount(s) of the credit(s) claimed.
- Complete Form 8867 truthfully and accurately and complete the actions

described on Form 8867 for any applicable credit(s) claimed and HOH filing status, if claimed.

- Submit Form 8867 in the manner required.
- Keep all five of the following records for 3 years from the latest of the dates specified.
  - A copy of Form 8867.
  - The applicable worksheet(s) or your own worksheet(s) for any credits claimed.
  - Copies of any taxpayer documents you may have relied upon to determine eligibility for the credit(s) and/or HOH filing status and to compute the amount(s) of the credit(s).
  - A record of how, when, and from whom the information used to prepare Form 8867 and the applicable worksheet(s) was obtained.
  - A record of any additional information you relied upon, including questions you asked and the taxpayer's responses, to determine the taxpayer's eligibility for the credit(s) and/or HOH filing status and to compute the amount(s) of the credit(s).

**Requirement #1: Form 8867, Paid Preparer's Due Diligence Checklist Appealing After an Examination**

Form 8867 covers the EIC, the CTC/ACTC/ODC, the AOTC, and/or HOH filing status. You should check the boxes corresponding to all benefits actually claimed on the return that you prepared.

Only paid tax return preparers should complete this form.

If you were paid to prepare a return for any taxpayer claiming the EIC, the CTC/ACTC/ODC, the AOTC, and/or HOH filing status, you must complete Form 8867 and meet the other due diligence requirements described later in Purpose of Form.

Form 8867 must be filed with the return.

Form 8867 must be filed with the taxpayer's return or amended return claiming the EIC, the CTC/ACTC/ODC, the AOTC, and/or HOH filing status.

**Signing tax return preparers.**

If you are the paid tax return preparer signing the return and you are filing the return electronically, file the completed Form 8867 electronically with the return.

If you are the paid tax return preparer signing the return and you are not electronically filing the return or mailing the return to the IRS for the taxpayer, provide the completed Form 8867 to the taxpayer with instructions to file this form with his or her return.

If you are the paid tax return preparer signing the return and you are mailing the return to the IRS for the taxpayer (which should only be done after the taxpayer has reviewed and signed the paper return), mail the completed Form 8867 to the IRS with the return.

**Non-signing tax return preparers.**

If you are the paid tax return preparer for any of the credits and/or HOH filing status covered by Form 8867, but you are not required to sign the return as a preparer, provide the signing tax return preparer the completed form in either electronic or paper format.

You can find rules regarding who is a signing tax return preparer and a non-signing tax return preparer in Regulations section 301.7701-15. If you are the only paid tax return preparer for the taxpayer's return, you are the signing tax return preparer and

must sign the return as preparer. Failure to sign the return when required may subject you to a penalty.

**Multiple Forms 8867 for one return.**

Form 8867 must be completed by a paid tax return preparer responsible for a taxpayer's claim of the EIC, the CTC/ACTC/ODC, the AOTC, and/or HOH filing status; therefore, there may be multiple Forms 8867 for one return or amended return. If there are multiple Forms 8867 for a paper return, attach all Forms 8867 to the return to be submitted to the IRS. If there are multiple Forms 8867 for an e-filed return, e-file will accept transmission of up to four Forms 8867. All Forms 8867 must be retained.

**Requirement #2: Compute The Credits on The Required Worksheets**

You can find the worksheets for the EIC and the CTC/ACTC/ODC in the Instructions for Forms 1040 and 1040-SR and in the Instructions for Form 1040-NR. The ACTC worksheet can also be found in the instructions for Forms 1040-PR and 1040-SS. You can find the AOTC worksheet in the Instructions for Form 8863.

Completion of these forms, schedules, and worksheets assists you in determining the taxpayer's eligibility for the credit and the correct amount of the credit and is required under the due diligence requirements set forth in Treasury Regulations.

### Requirement #3: Apply The Knowledge Requirement

As a paid tax return preparer, when determining the taxpayer's eligibility to claim a credit and/or HOH filing status and to determine the amount of a credit claimed on a return or claim for refund, you must not use information that you know, or have reason to know, is incorrect. You may not ignore the implications of information provided to or known by you, and you must make reasonable inquiries if the information provided to you appears to be incorrect, inconsistent, or incomplete. You must make reasonable inquiries if a reasonable and well-informed tax return preparer, knowledgeable in the tax law, would conclude that the information provided to you appears to be incorrect, inconsistent, or incomplete. You also must contemporaneously document in your files any reasonable inquiries made and the responses to these inquiries.

You must know the tax law for each credit and/or HOH filing status claimed on a return or claim for refund you prepare and use that knowledge to ask your client the right questions to get all the relevant facts to determine your client's eligibility to claim the credit(s) and/or HOH filing status and to compute the amount(s) of any credit(s) claimed.

**Gathering Facts from the Taxpayer:**

- Are these your foster sons or adopted sons? If so, were the children placed in your home for foster care by an authorized placement agency or court order or were they lawfully placed in your home for adoption?
- How long did the children live with you during the tax year?
- If the taxpayer is not the parent, did any other relative also reside with these children for more than half the year?
- How much did you charge to care for each lawn?
- Do you have records of the amount of money you received from lawn work?
- Did you have any expenses for lawn mowing equipment, fuel, or other supplies for your business? If not, how did you provide lawn care services?
- How many lawns did you take care of?

**Requirement #4: Preparer Record Keeping Compliance Requirements**

- You must keep records for 3 years from the latest of the following dates.
- The due date of the tax return (not including extensions).
- The date the return was filed (if you are a signing tax return preparer electronically filing the return).
- The date the return was presented to the taxpayer for signature (if you are a signing tax return preparer not electronically filing the return).
- The date you submitted to the signing tax return preparer the part of the return for which you were responsible (if you are a non-signing tax return preparer).

- These records may be kept on paper or electronically in the manner described in Rev. Proc. 97-22 (or later update).

The following are examples of documents that you may rely on to determine a taxpayer's eligibility to claim the credit(s), and/or HOH filing status, and the amount(s) of any credit(s) claimed.

1. Residency of a Qualifying Child
2. School records or statements.
3. Landlord or a property management statement.
4. Health care provider statement.
5. Medical records.
6. Child Care provider records.
7. Placement agency statement.
8. Social service records or statements.
9. Place of worship statement.
10. Indian tribal official statement.

## Disability of Qualifying Child
- Statement of medical doctor.
- Statement of another health care provider.
- Statement of social services agency or program statement.

## Schedule C
- Business license.
- Forms 1099.
- Records of gross receipts provided by the taxpayer.
- Taxpayer's summary of income or summary of income provided by taxpayer.
- Records of expenses provided by the taxpayer.
- Taxpayer's summary of expenses or summary of expenses provided by taxpayer.
- Bank statements to show income and expenses.

| Common EITC Errors | |
| --- | --- |
| Claiming a child who does not meet all the qualifying child tests: Relationship, Residency, Age, and Joint Return | We find most of the errors occur because the child is not related to the taxpayer in one of the listed relationships or the child didn't have the same main home as the taxpayer for the half of the tax year (residency test). |
| More than one person claiming the same child | This error often occurs because the child lived with more than one person for more than half of the tax year. But, sometimes, a taxpayer claims a child who didn't live with the taxpayer for more than half of the tax year. |
| Social Security Number or last name mismatches | Look at the Social Security card of everyone listed on your return to make sure the name and number of each person matches the records of the Social Security Administration. |
| Filing as a single or head of household when married | Unsure about your tax filing status? Use the EITC Assistant to find out! Or use the Spanish version of the EITC Assistant |
| Over- or under-reporting of income or expenses | Be sure you have all your Forms W-2, W-2G, 1099-MISC, and all the other relevant records of your income, even if not reported on a form, before you file your return. And you need to report all income you earn from running or owning a business or farm and deduct all allowable expenses. |

## Most Common AOTC Errors

- Students listed as a dependent or spouse on another tax return
- Students who don't have a Form 1098-T
- Students who are not paying qualified education expense

## The Most Common Child Tax Credit Errors

- Claiming a child who is not a qualifying child
- Married taxpayers who incorrectly file as single or head of household
- Income-reporting errors

## New Credit for Other Dependents (ODC)

This credit is for individuals with a dependent who meets additional conditions. This credit is in addition to the credit for child and dependent care expenses (on Schedule 3 (Form 1040 or 1040-SR), line 2, or Form 1040-NR, line 47) and the earned income credit (on Form 1040 or 1040-SR, line 18a).

The maximum amount you can claim for the credit is $500 for each dependent who qualifies for the ODC.

In addition to being a qualifying person for the ODC (defined earlier), the person must have an SSN, ITIN, or ATIN issued to the dependent on or before the due date of the return (including extensions).

## New Credit for Other Dependents (ODC)

Qualifying Person for the ODC - A person qualifies you for the ODC if the person meets all of the following conditions.
   A. The person is claimed as a dependent on your return.
   B. The person cannot be used by you to claim the CTC or ACTC.
   C. The person was a U.S. citizen, U.S. national, or U.S. resident alien.

## Penalties For Failure to Exercise Due Diligence

The penalty for failure to be diligent has increased. For returns filed in calendar year 2023 is $560.00 for each failure. The penalty for returns filed in calendar year 2024 is $600.00. For example, for tax year 2024 if you are paid to prepare a return claiming the EIC, the CTC/ACTC/ODC, the AOTC, and/or HOH filing status, and you fail to meet the due diligence requirements for all of these credits, you could be subject to a penalty of $2,400.

- The IRS can also penalize an employer or employing firm if an employee fails to comply with the due diligence requirements. There are specific circumstances when an employer is subject to the due diligence penalty (reference: Treasury Regulations 1.6695.2(c)).

- If the IRS examines your client's return and denies all or a part of the EITC, the CTC/ACTC/ODC, the AOTC, or HOH filing status, your client must pay back any amount in error with interest.
- May be subject to the 20 percent accuracy-related penalty and the 75 percent fraud penalty
- May need to file Form 8862, Information to Claim Certain Credits After Disallowance.
- May be banned from claiming one or more of the credits for the next two years if we find the error is because of reckless or intentional disregard of the rules.
- May be banned from claiming one or more of the credits for the next ten years if we find the error is because of fraud.

**The following are examples of situations when you should ask additional questions to meet your due diligence knowledge requirement:**

1. A client wants to claim head of household

filing status and claim his niece and nephew for the EITC and the CTC.

    a. You should ask enough questions to determine whether each child meets the requirements to be a qualifying child of your client, including reasonable inquiries about the children's residency, the client's relationship to the children, the children's income, the sources of support for the children, and the client's contribution to the payment of costs related to operating the household.

2. An 18-year-old client with an infant has $8,000 in earned income and states she lived with her parents during part of the year. She wants to claim the infant as a qualifying child for the EITC and the CTC.

    a. This information seems incomplete because your 18-year-old client lives with her parents and earns $8,000. You must ask additional questions to determine whether your client is the qualifying child of her parents. Be sure to review all tests to determine who is eligible to claim each credit.

3. A client has two qualifying children and wants to claim the EITC. She tells you she had a Schedule C business and earned $10,000 in income and had no expenses.

    a. This information appears incomplete because it is unusual that someone who is self-employed has no business expenses. You must ask additional reasonable questions to determine if the business exists and whether the information about her income and expenses is correct.

4. A 22-year-old client wants to claim two sons, ages 10 and 11, as qualifying children for the EITC.

   a. You must make additional reasonable inquiries regarding the relationship between your client and the children, because the age of the client seems inconsistent with the ages of the children claimed as your client's sons.

5. A 32-year-old client indicates he's been going to college for many years and would like to claim the AOTC. He provides a Form 1098- T, Tuition Statement, showing $4,000 received for tuition and that he was at least a half-time undergraduate student.

   a. You must ask more questions. The Form 1098-T is a good indicator that your client is eligible for the AOTC, but it does not contain all the information needed to determine eligibility for the credit or to compute the amount of the credit. You must also find out whether your client received any scholarships, how and when the expenses were paid, whether your client has a felony drug conviction, and whether your client claimed the AOTC or the Hope Credit previously and, if so, for how many years.

6. A client wants to claim the ODC for his three children. Your client is a resident alien. The children all have ITINs and lived part of the year outside the U.S.

    a. You must ask questions to determine whether each child is related to your client, meets the U.S. residency requirement, and has an ITIN issued on or before the due date of the return.

## Identity Theft

Tax preparers play a critical role in assisting individual and business clients who are victims of tax-related identity theft. The IRS is working hard to prevent and detect identity theft as well as reduce the time it takes to resolve these cases.

## What is tax-related identity theft?

Tax-related identity theft occurs when someone uses a stolen Social Security number to file a tax return claiming a fraudulent refund. Thieves may also use stolen Employer Identification numbers to create false Forms W-2 to support refund fraud schemes.

## Warning signs for individual clients

Your client's SSN may be compromised, putting them at risk when:

• The IRS rejects their e-file return, and the code indicates the taxpayer's SSN was already used, or They notice activity on their account, or they receive IRS notices regarding a tax return after all tax issues were resolved, refund received or account balances paid, or

• They receive an IRS notice indicating they earned wages from an employer unknown to them.

Remember: You must have a power of attorney on file and authenticate your identity before an IRS customer service representative can provide you with any taxpayer information.

### Assisting victims of identity theft

The Federal Trade Commission, the lead federal agency for identity theft, recommends these steps for victims:
1. File a complaint and get a recovery plan at IdentityTheft.gov.
2. Place a fraud alert on the victim's credit report by contacting one of the three major credit bureaus.

3. Review the victim's credit report and consider closing any financial or credit card accounts that can't be confirmed.

### IRS victim assistance

In addition to FTC recommendations, you should take the following steps if a client's SSN is compromised, and they suspect or know they're a victim of tax-related identity theft:

• Respond promptly to IRS notices.

• Complete Form 14039, Identity Theft Affidavit, if

we rejected their e-file return and the reject code indicates a duplicate filing under their SSN, or you're instructed to do so. Attach Form 14039 to their paper return and mail according to instructions. This form allows us to put an indicator on the client's tax records for questionable activity.

• Clients should continue to file returns and pay taxes, even if it must be done on paper while we research their case.

## Warning signs for business clients

• Your client's business return is processed as an amended return, but they haven't filed a return for that year.

• Your client receives IRS notices about fictitious employees.

• Your client detects activity related to or receives IRS notices regarding a closed or dormant business after they paid all account balances. If any of the above conditions affect your client, please refer them to irs.gov/BusinessIDT.

# POP QUIZ & ANSWER SHEET
# Due Diligence & Identity Theft

## POP QUIZ

Test your knowledge on *Due Diligence & Identity Theft* by answering the questions below. The answer sheet may be found at the end of the Pop Quiz.

**Q1: What form covers the EIC, the CTC/ACTC/ODC, the AOTC, and/or HOH filing status? Only paid tax return preparers should complete this form.**
- A.   Form 8821
- B.   Form 8822
- C.   Form 2848
- D.   Form 8867

**Q2: You must use _____ ensure the computation of credits is done correctly even if you are using tax software.**
- A.   Procedures
- B.   Worksheets
- C.   Publications
- D.   Internal Revenue Manual

**Q3: As a paid tax return preparer, when determining the taxpayer's eligibility to claim a credit and/or HOH filing status and to determine the amount of a credit claimed on a return or claim for refund, you must not use information that you know, or have reason to know, is incorrect. You may not ignore the implications of information provided to or known by you.**

**What must the tax preparer do if he knows that the information provided is incorrect?**

A.  He must make reasonable inquiries if the information provided to him appears to be incorrect, inconsistent, or incomplete. He must make reasonable inquiries if a reasonable and well-informed tax return preparer, knowledgeable in the tax law, would conclude that the information provided to him appears to be incorrect, inconsistent, or incomplete. He also must contemporaneously document in your files any reasonable inquiries made and the responses to these inquiries.

B.  He must make reasonable inquiries and if they are still inconsistent document the answers and continue with the tax preparation filing.

C.  He must make reasonable inquiries if the information provided to him appears to be incorrect and refer the client to another preparer because it is his moral duty to do what the law states.

D.  He must make reasonable inquiries if the information provided to him appears to be incorrect, inconsistent, or incomplete. He must report his client to the IRS.

**Q4: You must keep records for 3 years from the latest of the following dates, except:**

A.    For a paper return, the date the return was presented to the client for signature

B.    The due date of the tax return

C.    The date the tax return was electronically filed

D.    The date you started preparing the taxpayers clients

**Q5: The following are examples of documents for Residency of a Qualifying Child that you may rely on to determine a taxpayer's eligibility to claim the credits, except:**

A.    A rental property lease

B.    Records for school or childcare enrollment

C.    The dependent's birth certificate

D.    Divorce decree, separation agreement or custody order

**Q6: The following are examples of documents for Disability of Qualifying Child that you may rely on to determine a taxpayer's eligibility to claim the credit, except:**

A.    Statement of Medical Doctor

B.    Statement of Place of Worship

C.    Statement of Other Health Care Provider

D.    Statement of Social Services Agency or Program Statement

**Q7: Claiming a child who does not meet all the qualifying child tests: relationship, residency, age and joint return. This is an example of what common error?**

    A.    Child Tax Credit Error

    B.    AOTC Error

    C.    New Credit Error

    D.    EITC Error

**Q8: Students listed as a dependent or spouse on another tax return. This is an example of what common error?**

    A.    Child Tax Credit Error

    B.    AOTC Error

    C.    New Credit Error

    D.    EITC Error

**Q9:** Kelly, an Enrolled Agent, failed to perform due diligence on a taxpayer's return and complete Form 8867 Paid Preparer's Due Diligence Checklist for credit CTC, EITC, AOTC, and HOH. Per the knowledge requirement of IRC §6695, how much penalty could Kelly face?

    A. $1120

    B. $2240

    C. $1680

    D. $560

**Q10: The AOTC is only available for ___ years of post-secondary education.**

    A.    Five years

    B.    Four years

    C.    Three years

    D.    Two years

### Q11: What is a Tax-Related Identity Theft?

    A.    When someone steals your personal name and social security number to file a fraudulent tax return

    B.    When someone sends an email that contains a virus that takes over your computer

    C.    When someone calls you and pretends to be from human resources to get you to tell them your social security number and date of birth

    D.    All of the above

### Q12: All are signs of Identity Theft, except:

    A.    You get a tax transcript in the mail that you did not request.

    B.    You get a Statement of Account from your credit card company to your address.

    C.    You get an IRS notice that an online account has been created in your name.

    D.    You get a letter from the IRS inquiring about a suspicious tax return that you did not file.

### Q13: All are warning signs a business's EIN has been compromised, except:

    A.    The business receives IRS notices regarding a dissolved business entity

    B.    The business receives IRS notices about non-existent employees

    C.    The business receives IRS notice of demand for payment for payroll taxes the owner forgot to pay

    D.    The business return is accepted as an amended return, but the business has not filed an original return for the year

**Q14: All are examples of a client's SSN being compromised, except:**

    A.    The IRS rejects their e-file return, and the code indicates the taxpayer's SSN was already used.

    B.    They notice activity on their account, or they receive IRS notices regarding a tax return after all tax issues were resolved, refund received, or account balances paid.

    C.    They receive an IRS notice indicating they earned wages from an employer unknown to them.

    D.    They receive a tax transcript their tax professional ordered on their behalf to file a past due tax return.

**Q15: It is a scam typically carried out through unsolicited email and/or websites that pose as legitimate sites and lure unsuspecting victims to provide personal and financial information.**

    A.    Competition Scam
    B.    Phishing
    C.    Computer Hacking
    D.    Spade Phishing

**Q16: All are ways to protect clients from phishing, except:**

    A.    Use strong unique passwords preferably phrases
    B.    Take emails from a familiar source at face value
    C.    Use security software to help defend against malware and viruses
    D.    Use verbal confirmations by phone if you receive an email from a new client sending you tax information or requesting a last-minute change to their refund destination

**Q17: This type of attack is when cybercriminals will pose as company executives in order to obtain sensitive personal information such as name, date of birth, and**

**payroll information.**

    A.    Cyber Attack
    B.    Phishing Attack
    C.    Social Engineering Attack
    D.    Spear Attack

**Q18: All are ways you can avoid being a victim of fraud, except:**

    A.    Pay attention to URLs of a website
    B.    Verify by phone suspicious emails for legitimacy
    C.    Click on all links within an email from an unknown source to verify it is legitimate
    D.    Avoid revealing personal or financial information in an email

**Q19: It involves victims being bombarded with false alarms and fictitious threats. Users are deceived to think their system is infected with malware, prompting them to install software that has no real benefit (other than for the perpetrator) or is malware itself.**

    A.    Pretexting
    B.    Social Engineering Attacks
    C.    Baiting
    D.    Scareware

**Q20: All are true regarding Identity Protection Pins, except:**

    A.    All taxpayers may apply for an identity protection personal identification number
    B.    The IP PIN is valid for two years
    C.    An IP Pin is a six-digit number that helps to prevent misuse of a taxpayer's social security number
    D.    If the taxpayer attempts to file an electronic return without his IP PIN it will return rejected

# ANSWER SHEET
# Due Diligence & Identity Theft

**Q1: What form covers the EIC, the CTC/ACTC/ODC, the AOTC, and/or HOH filing status? Only paid tax return preparers should complete this form.**

A. Form 8821
B. Form 8822
C. Form 2848
D. Form 8867

**Answer:** D. Form 8867

**Explanation:** Form 8867, Paid Preparer's Due Diligence Checklist, is the form that paid tax return preparers must complete to ensure that they are meeting the due diligence requirements for claiming the Earned Income Credit (EIC), Child Tax Credit (CTC), Additional Child Tax Credit (ACTC), Other Dependent Credit (ODC), American Opportunity Tax Credit (AOTC), and Head of Household (HOH) filing status.

**Q2: You must use _____ to ensure the computation of credits is done correctly even if you are using tax software.**

A. Procedures
B. Worksheets
C. Publications
D. Internal Revenue Manual

**Answer:** B. Worksheets

**Explanation:** Worksheets must be used to ensure the computation of credits is done correctly, even if tax software is being used. Worksheets help to methodically verify and document the calculations.

**Q3: As a paid tax return preparer, when determining the taxpayer's eligibility to claim a credit and/or HOH filing status and to determine the amount of a credit claimed on a return or claim for refund, you must not use information that you know, or have reason to know, is incorrect. You may not ignore the implications of information provided to or known by you. What must the tax preparer do if he knows that the information provided is incorrect?**

A. He must make reasonable inquiries if the information provided to him appears to be incorrect, inconsistent, or incomplete. He must make reasonable inquiries if a reasonable and well-informed tax return preparer, knowledgeable in the tax law, would conclude that the information provided to him appears to be incorrect, inconsistent, or incomplete. He also must contemporaneously document in your files any reasonable inquiries made and the responses to these inquiries.
B. He must make reasonable inquiries and if they are still inconsistent document the answers and continue with the tax preparation filing.
C. He must make reasonable inquiries if the information provided to him appears to be incorrect and refer the client to another preparer because it is his moral duty to do what the law states.
D. He must make reasonable inquiries if the information provided to him appears to be incorrect, inconsistent, or incomplete. He must report his client to the IRS.

**Answer:** A. He must make reasonable inquiries if the information provided to him appears to be incorrect, inconsistent, or incomplete. He must make reasonable inquiries if a reasonable and well-informed tax return preparer, knowledgeable in the tax law, would conclude that the information provided to him appears to be incorrect, inconsistent, or incomplete. He also must contemporaneously document in your files any reasonable inquiries made and the responses to these inquiries.

**Explanation:** The tax preparer must make reasonable inquiries and document these inquiries and responses to ensure the accuracy and completeness of the information used to determine eligibility for credits and HOH filing status.

**Q4: You must keep records for 3 years from the latest of the following dates, except:**

A. For a paper return, the date the return was presented to the client for signature
B. The due date of the tax return
C. The date the tax return was electronically filed
D. The date you started preparing the taxpayers clients

**Answer:** D. The date you started preparing the taxpayers clients

**Explanation:** The record-keeping requirement does not depend on the date you started preparing the tax return but rather on the dates associated with the completion and submission of the return.

**Q5: The following are examples of documents for Residency of a Qualifying Child that you may rely on to determine a taxpayer's eligibility to claim the credits, except:**

A. A rental property lease
B. Records for school or childcare enrollment
C. The dependent's birth certificate
D. Divorce decree, separation agreement or custody order

**Answer:** C. The dependent's birth certificate

**Explanation:** A birth certificate proves relationship but not residency. Documents like rental property leases, school records, and custody orders can provide evidence of residency.

**Q6: The following are examples of documents for Disability of Qualifying Child that you may rely on to determine a taxpayer's eligibility to claim the credit, except:**

A. Statement of Medical Doctor
B. Statement of Place of Worship
C. Statement of Other Health Care Provider
D. Statement of Social Services Agency or Program Statement

**Answer:** B. Statement of Place of Worship

**Explanation:** Statements from medical doctors, other health care providers, and social services agencies are appropriate for verifying a disability, but a statement from a place of worship is not.

**Q7: Claiming a child who does not meet all the qualifying child tests: relationship, residency, age and joint return. This is an example of what common error?**

A. Child Tax Credit Error
B. AOTC Error
C. New Credit Error
D. EITC Error

**Answer:** D. EITC Error

**Explanation:** The Earned Income Tax Credit (EITC) requires that the qualifying child meet tests for relationship, residency, age, and joint return. Failing to meet any of these test's results in an EITC error.

**Q8: Students listed as a dependent or spouse on another tax return. This is an example of what common error?**

A. Child Tax Credit Error
B. AOTC Error
C. New Credit Error
D. EITC Error

**Answer:** B. AOTC Error

**Explanation:** Claiming the American Opportunity Tax Credit (AOTC) for students listed as a dependent or spouse on another tax return is an AOTC error.

**Q9: Kelly, an Enrolled Agent, failed to perform due diligence on a taxpayer's return and complete Form 8867 Paid Preparer's Due Diligence Checklist for credit CTC, EITC, AOTC, and HOH. Per the knowledge requirement of IRC §6695, how much penalty could Kelly face?**

A. $1120
B. $2240
C. $1680
D. $560

**Answer:** D. $560

**Explanation:** The penalty for failing to meet the due diligence requirements, including completing Form 8867, is $560 per failure per return as per IRC §6695(g).

**Q10: The AOTC is only available for _____ years of post-secondary education.**

A. Five years
B. Four years
C. Three years
D. Two years

**Answer:** B. Four years

**Explanation:** The American Opportunity Tax Credit (AOTC) is available for the first four years of post-secondary education.


**Q11: What is a Tax-Related Identity Theft?**

A. When someone steals your personal name and social security number to file a fraudulent tax return
B. When someone sends an email that contains a virus that takes over your computer
C. When someone calls you and pretends to be from human resources to get you to tell them your social security number and date of birth
D. All of the above

**Answer:** A. When someone steals your personal name and social security number to file a fraudulent tax return

**Explanation:** Tax-Related Identity Theft occurs when someone uses your personal information to file a fraudulent tax return in your name.

**Q12: All are signs of Identity Theft, except:**

A. You get a tax transcript in the mail that you did not request.
B. You get a Statement of Account from your credit card company to your address.
C. You get an IRS notice that an online account has been created in your name.
D. You get a letter from the IRS inquiring about a suspicious tax return that you did not file.

**Answer:** B. You get a Statement of Account from your credit card company to your address.

**Explanation:** A Statement of Account from your credit card company is not necessarily a sign of identity theft, whereas unsolicited tax transcripts, account creation notices, and IRS inquiries about suspicious returns are clear signs.

**Q13: All are warning signs a business's EIN has been compromised, except:**

A. The business receives IRS notices regarding a dissolved business entity
B. The business receives IRS notices about non-existent employees
C. The business receives IRS notice of demand for payment for payroll taxes the owner forgot to pay
D. The business return is accepted as an amended return, but the business has not filed an original return for the year

**Answer:** C. The business receives IRS notice of demand for payment for payroll taxes the owner forgot to pay

**Explanation:** Receiving an IRS notice for unpaid payroll taxes may be a result of legitimate business oversight, whereas the other options indicate possible identity theft or misuse of the EIN.

**Q14: All are examples of a client's SSN being compromised, except:**

A. The IRS rejects their e-file return, and the code indicates the taxpayer's SSN was already used.
B. They notice activity on their account, or they receive IRS notices regarding a tax return after all tax issues were resolved, refund received, or account balances paid.
C. They receive an IRS notice indicating they earned wages from an employer unknown to them.
D. They receive a tax transcript their tax professional ordered on their behalf to file a past due tax return.

**Answer:** D. They receive a tax transcript their tax professional ordered on their behalf to file a past due tax return.

**Explanation:** Receiving a tax transcript ordered by their tax professional is not indicative of SSN compromise, unlike the other scenarios which point to possible identity theft.

**Q15: It is a scam typically carried out through unsolicited email and/or websites that pose as legitimate sites and lure unsuspecting victims to provide personal and financial information.**

A. Competition Scam
B. Phishing
C. Computer Hacking
D. Spade Phishing

**Answer:** B. Phishing

**Explanation:** Phishing is a scam where perpetrators pose as legitimate entities to lure victims into providing personal and financial information through unsolicited emails or websites.

**Q16: All are ways to protect clients from phishing, except:**

A. Use strong unique passwords preferably phrase
B. Take emails from a familiar source at face value
C. Use security software to help defend against malware and viruses
D. Use verbal confirmations by phone if you receive an email from a new client sending you tax information or requesting a last-minute change to their refund destination

**Answer:** B. Take emails from a familiar source at face value

**Explanation:** Taking emails from familiar sources at face value can be risky as they might be spoofed. It is always important to verify the legitimacy of emails, even if they appear to come from familiar sources.

**Q17: This type of attack is when cybercriminals will pose as company executives in order to obtain sensitive personal information such as name, date of birth, and payroll information.**

A. Cyber Attack
B. Phishing Attack
C. Social Engineering Attack
D. Spear Attack

**Answer:** C. Social Engineering Attack

**Explanation:** Social Engineering Attacks involve criminals posing as trusted individuals, such as company executives, to obtain sensitive information.

**Q18: All are ways you can avoid being a victim of fraud, except:**

A. Pay attention to URLs of a website
B. Verify by phone suspicious emails for legitimacy
C. Click on all links within an email from an unknown source to verify it is legitimate
D. Avoid revealing personal or financial information in an email

**Answer:** C. Click on all links within an email from an unknown source to verify it is legitimate

**Explanation:** Clicking on links in emails from unknown sources can lead to phishing or malware attacks. It is better to verify the source and avoid clicking suspicious links.

**Q19: It involves victims being bombarded with false alarms and fictitious threats. Users are deceived to think their system is infected with malware, prompting them to install software that has no real benefit (other than for the perpetrator) or is malware itself.**

A. Pretexting
B. Social Engineering Attacks
C. Baiting
D. Scareware

**Answer:** D. Scareware

**Explanation:** Scareware involves deceiving users with false alarms about malware infections to prompt them to install unnecessary or malicious software.

**Q20: All are true regarding Identity Protection Pins, except:**

A. All taxpayers may apply for an identity protection personal identification number
B. The IP PIN is valid for two years
C. An IP Pin is a six-digit number that helps to prevent misuse of a taxpayer's social security number
D. If the taxpayer attempts to file an electronic return without his IP PIN it will return rejected

**Answer:** B. The IP PIN is valid for two years

**Explanation:** An IP PIN is valid for only one calendar year and must be renewed each year.

# ABOUT CERTIFYIBLE.COM

**Certifyible.com** is a leading edtech platform designed for tax and accounting professionals. With a robust curriculum and comprehensive resources, it empowers CPAs, EAs, and tax attorneys through high-quality continuing education and practical training. Certifyible.com boasts a community of over 6,000 learners across 13 countries, primarily in the US. It offers a wide range of courses, coaching, and business development tools, helping professionals to start, grow, and scale their firms successfully. The platform's commitment to excellence is evident in its IRS-approved courses and a strong track record of facilitating significant revenue growth for its users.

Made in the USA
Las Vegas, NV
04 December 2024

13338068R00144